CHRIST

God's

Final

Word

to

Man

D1560363

CHRIST
God's Final
Word to Man

An Exposition
of the Epistle
to the Hebrews

Herman A. Hoyt

BMH Books
P.O. Box 544, Winona Lake, IN 46590

ISBN: 0-88469-009-01

COPYRIGHT 1974
BMH BOOKS
WINONA LAKE, INDIANA

Printed in U.S.A.

First printing, October, 1974
Second printing, July, 1982

Cover design by Mary Jane Fretz

DEDICATION

To my wife,
Harriet L. Hoyt,
who labors with me
in the Gospel

Foreword

Dr. Herman Hoyt presents to those interested in the study of the Book of Hebrews a well-outlined book. He takes the reader through one of the most important sections of the New Testament with the greatest of care. With this excellent material and an open Bible before you, there will be many happy hours of spiritual enlightenment and blessing. However, this study guide is not intended to answer all the questions with pages of material, but the reader will be delighted to find every portion of the book is covered. Each sentence is filled with meaningful and thought-provoking material. After reading a few pages, the student of the Scriptures will be impressed with the unique method of outlining.

Dr. Hoyt is well qualified to expound the Scriptures. His background in classroom teaching as well as his contact with people in Bible conferences and church services keeps him alert to the need for clear exposition of Biblical truth. His position as president of Grace Schools for many years speaks well of his acquaintance with teaching at its best.

The study guide itself is one of a series prepared by BMH Books to give the student material that will aid him in better knowing the Word of God. Hopefully, this knowledge will deepen his Christian faith. The study guides are each divided into thirteen chapters making them adaptable for use in Sunday School classes.

These BMH Books are being used in many Bible colleges and institutes as well as for informal group studies. However, the wide application does not exclude quiet meditation by persons who want help in their devotional studies.

—Charles W. Turner
Executive Editor, BMH Books

Table of
Contents

The
Authorship
of Hebrews

There is no more intriguing question among scholars than the authorship of the Epistle to the Hebrews. From very early times this has been an open question among close students of the letter, although among the rank and file within the Christian church it has been credited to just one man.

There are those who insist that it does not make any difference who wrote the book. It is argued that it is enough to know that the book is the inspired, eternal Word of God. To this, one must reply that there is a certain plausibility, but it extends only so far. For the human elements in the New Testament books were certainly divinely used. And just as in most human correspondence, the signature at the close throws its own light over the whole missive.

It may be, as some have suggested, that we shall never discover the identity of the author this side of heaven. But even that conclusion is uncertain. For as new evidence comes to light the whole picture may change. Within recent years archaeological discoveries bearing on this point are focusing the issue upon one man.

Some argue that the book was written anonymously, because no name is written into the body of the text. But it does not necessarily follow that the omission of the name means it is anonymous. In the case of this epistle it may be because the author is so well known it was not necessary for him to include it. The reading of 10:34 in the Authorized Version would support this, although the substitution of "them" for "me" and "my" in the Revised Version disposes of this text. However, the reading of 13:19, 22-25 is certainly clear. But if Paul is the writer, the omission of the name may be because of the strong Jewish prejudice against him. It has been suggested, though, that inasmuch as the writer, perhaps Paul, is presenting Christ as the great Apostle to the Jews (3:1), he purposely avoids making any reference to himself so as not to detract in any way from the One he is presenting.

Regardless of anonymity of the epistle, numerous suggestions have been made through the years. Paul is perhaps the earliest suggestion of the church and remains to this day the most popular choice. Barnabas comes next, though hardly a man with the strength of personality as suggested by the epistle (Gal. 2:13). Clement of Rome is scarcely more than a suggestion. Luke too has been proposed, and if not the writer, then perhaps he is the amanuensis. Apollos, Aquila, Priscilla, Mark, Philip the deacon, and Aristion have all come into mind on this question.

Internal evidence, however, to the writer, supports the Pauline authorship of this great epistle. The author is without doubt a Jew, if one can draw any valid conclusion from the way he identifies himself with the people to whom he is writing (1:2; 3:1; 4:1; 8:1; 9:24; 10:15; 11:40; 12:1). And he is most certainly a Christian, even as his readers, judging from the statements which could be applied to no others (3:1, 6; 4:14-16; 10:23-25).

While the above could be true of others as well as Paul, the moment he speaks of Timothy as a brother (13:23), and writes from Italy where Paul once was (13:24), and closes his epistle in the characteristic Pauline style, "Grace be with you all" (13:25), one is made to think of Paul. As one notes the order and arrangement of the argument, beginning first with doctrine and then shifting to duty, he is made to think of other Pauline epistles. And surely no one was more firmly entrenched in Judaism than Paul, and once rescued, would be better fitted to write to people in the same peril (Gal. 1:11-16).

The external evidence in favor of Pauline authorship is even more convincing. The early church held almost universally to this position. A host of eminent church fathers can

13

be cited, such as Clement of Alexandria, Pantaenus, Origen, Athanasius, Jerome, Augustine. While tradition cannot be cited as conclusive proof, still it must not be entirely ignored.

Three orders of the New Testament books place Hebrews among Paul's epistles. The Greek order places it between II Thessalonians and I Timothy. The Latin order is that followed in the Authorized Version and there it is the concluding book in Paul's collection. The Beatty Papyri were discovered in Egypt and to the amazement of everyone, Hebrews is placed immediately after Romans.

In Paul's second letter to the Thessalonians he declares that his salutation is affixed at the close of every epistle (3:17). And if the statement, "Grace be with you all," is it, then Hebrews falls in the class with all the known Pauline epistles.

A textual connection between three epistles is certainly a curious coincidence, if all three epistles are not from one mind and one hand. Paul liked the text in Habakkuk 2:4, "The just shall live by his faith." It provides the basis for Romans (1:17), Galatians (3:11), and Hebrews (10:38). Romans expounds the first two words, "the just"; Galatians, the second two, "shall live"; and Hebrews, the final two, "by faith."

Could any epistle other than Hebrews more elaborately expand the yearning of Paul for his people according to the flesh, as expressed briefly in Romans? "I say the truth in Christ, I lie not, my conscience also bearing me witness in the Holy Ghost, that I have great heaviness and continual sorrow in my heart. For I could wish that myself were accursed from Christ for my brethren, my kinsmen according to the flesh" (Rom. 9:1-3).

Peter seems to give the crowning proof for the Pauline authorship of Hebrews. In his first epistle he affirms that he writes to Christian Jews of the dispersion (I Peter 1:1-2). In his second epistle he insists that he is now writing the second epistle to the same group (II Peter 3:1). Then as he moves toward the close of this second epistle he writes, "And account that the longsuffering of our Lord is salvation; even as our beloved brother Paul also according to the wisdom given unto him hath written unto you; as also in all his epistles, speaking in them of these things; in which are some things hard to be understood, which they that are unlearned and unstable wrest, as they do also the other scriptures, unto their own destruction" (II Peter 3:15-16).

Two things seem to be quite clear, namely, that Paul wrote to Christian Jews, and the letter he wrote is Scripture. Is there any one of his letters directed to Hebrew Christians, unless it be the Epistle to the Hebrews? And if it is not the Book of Hebrews, then certainly a letter of his, which is Scripture, has been lost, and we do not have all the New Testament. One is therefore driven to one conclusion: Hebrews must be a letter from his own Spirit-directed hand.

OUTLINE OF THE EPISTLE TO THE HEBREWS

Introduction 1:1-4
1. The revelation in the Son. 1:1—2a
2. The salvation through the Son. 1:2b—3
3. The exaltation of the Son. 1:4

1A. THE POSITION OF CHRIST: DEALING WITH HIS PERSON. 1:5—4:16

Key words: "Son" (1:2); "Person" (1:3).
Question: "Who Is Jesus Christ?"
- 1b. His position in Revelation as Prophet (cf. 1:2 with 3:1). 1:5—2:4
- 2b. His position in Redemption as Priest (cf. 2:10). 2:5-18
- 3b. His position in Reconciliation as Prophet and Priest (cf. 3:1). 3—4

2A. THE PERFECTION OF CHRIST: DEALING WITH HIS OFFICE. 5—7

Key words: "ordained" (5:1); "perfect" (5:9).
Question: "What is Christ like?"
- 1b. The description of the elements of Perfection (5:9). 5
- 2b. The confirmation of the elements of Perfection (6:16). 6
- 3b. The illustration of the elements of Perfection (7:11). 7

3A. THE PROVISION OF CHRIST: DEALING WITH HIS MINISTRY. 8—10

Key words: "minister" (8:2); "offer" (8:3).
Question: "What did Christ do for men?"
- 1b. The provision of a better covenant (8:6). 8
- 2b. The provision of a new sanctuary (9:11). 9
- 3b. The provision of one sacrifice (10:12). 10

4A. THE POSSESSION OF CHRIST: DEALING WITH HIS EXAMPLE. 11:1—13:23

Key words: "author and finisher" (12:2).
Question: "How can men possess the salvation in Christ?"
- 1b. The appropriation of Christ by faith (11:1). 11
- 2b. The perseverance in Christ by faith (12:1). 12
- 3b. The separation unto Christ by faith (13:13). 13

Conclusion 13:24-25

1

Introduction
and Position
of Christ

1. The epistle we are about to study occupies a unique *place* in the New Testament. For remarkable values, suggestive teaching, beauty of statement, perfection of system, and things hard to be understood, there is no writing in the New Testament more wonderful. It appeared at a time when it was most needed, and its value to believers has not diminished through the passing of centuries.

2. It is self-evident that the *people* to whom this was written were Hebrew Christians. But its teaching is for all Christians. The Hebrew people were specially chosen of God to be His instrument for reaching all nations. But they failed under the former covenant. During this final covenant, however, God planned to accomplish His purpose through Christian Hebrews. But at the very beginning it began to appear that He would fail of accomplishment. "For when for the time ye ought to be teachers, ye have need that one teach you again which be the first principles of the oracles of God" (Heb. 5:12).

3. The *problem* facing the Hebrew Christians of that day is the problem facing Christians today. And the problem had two sides. The doctrinal side was the very low view they held of the person of Christ, while the practical side was the persecutions they had to endure for Christ. It is significant, therefore, that the writer exhorts them to "consider the Apostle and High Priest of our profession, Christ Jesus" (Heb. 3:1), and again to "consider him that endured such contradiction of sinners against himself, lest ye be wearied and faint in your minds" (Heb. 12:3).

4. The writer therefore sets himself to the *purpose* of convincing his readers concerning the person of Christ and encouraging them to face persecution for Christ. Weighted as they were with centuries of Old Testament religion and rea-

soning, the writer must set forth *Christ as God's last word to man.* "God, who at sundry times and in divers manners spake in time past unto the fathers by the prophets, hath in these last days spoken unto us by his Son" (Heb. 1:1-2). It is therefore absolutely necessary to "See that ye refuse not him that speaketh. For if they escaped not who refused him that spake on earth, much more shall not we escape if we turn away from him that speaketh from heaven" (Heb. 12:25).

5. The writer adopts the following fourfold plan to accomplish his purpose with these Hebrew Christians, and with all Christians down through the centuries. In the first four chapters he presents the *Position* of Christ when looking at His person (key word—"person," 1:3). In chapters 5 through 7 it is the *Perfection* of Christ in His office as Priest (key word—"perfect," 5:9). In chapters 8, 9 and 10 the writer points to the *Provision* of Christ growing out of His ministry (key word—"minister" 8:2). And finally the *Possession* of Christ accomplished by faith is urged in the remaining chapters (key word—"faith," 11:1). Because of His supreme position (1—4), and absolute perfection (5—7), and indispensable provision (8—10), believers should make Him their personal possession by faith (11—13).

I. THE PREFACE TO THE ENTIRE EPISTLE (1:1-4).

The first four verses of this chapter constitute a sort of introduction or preface to the entire epistle, and they are so designed that they are called an epitome of the book, meaning that they are cut over the same pattern as the book. In these four verses all the truth of the entire book is condensed. The revelation in Christ (1:1-2) gives in condensed form the message of the first four chapters; the salvation in Christ (1:2-3) gives in the same way the message of chapters 5 through 10; and the exaltation of Christ (1:4) gives the message of chapters 11 through 13.

1. The *revelation* in Christ (1:1-2). "In time past" or former days describes the Old Testament contract, while "these last days" points to the New Testament. Hence there are just two great periods of revelation, the former or first, and the final or last. In both of these it is God who speaks to His people.

In the *former* covenant God spoke "at sundry times and in divers manners." This phrase describes the method God used to reveal himself to men. *"At sundry times"* means in fragmentary nature. It was in many portions and no one or all of the portions were perfect or complete. There was progress from one portion to another, but revelation never reached completeness. God spoke a little to Adam, and a little to Noah, and a little to Moses, and a little to the prophets, and so on. But revelation never reached completeness.

"In divers manners" describes the various ways in which God spoke to men in the former period. Sometimes it was the direct voice of God (Exod. 33:11); sometimes by writing (Exod. 31:18); at others it was by dreams (Gen. 40–41), or vision (Ezek. 1:1). God also used the spiritual life and experiences of His people (Psalms), the direct influence of the Holy Spirit (II Peter 1:21), or the natural world and miraculous events (Rom. 1:19-20). He also used typical things and historical events (I Cor. 10:6, 11).

But in the *final* covenant God spoke "in his Son." There was no difference between the Son and God. In the Son, God came near to His people. This was a personal revelation, lacking in no respect, absolutely infallible and authoritative, and hence the last word God will ever speak to men. Those who do not heed the message in the Son will have no hope.

2. The *salvation* in Christ (1:2-3). The latter part of

verse 2 and the first part of verse 3 set forth the *perfection* of Christ. His perfection *in relation to the universe* is threefold. "Heir of all things" presents Him at the consummation of the universe when He will receive everything as His own. "He made the worlds" points to the commencement of the universe. And "the worlds" or ages marks the continuation from the beginning to the end.

His perfection *within himself* has to do with His person and work. In His *person* He is "the brightness of his glory, and the express image of his person." This means that He is exactly the same as God for He is God. In His *work* He is always "upholding all things by the word of his power," with never a moment since the beginning of creation that He has not been performing this mighty work in the universe.

The latter part of verse 3 sets forth the *provision* of Christ,". . . when he had by himself purged our sins, sat down on the right hand of the Majesty on high." In order to perform this work, it was necessary for God the Son to come into the world He had made and redeem it. He did this and then returned on high indicating that He had completely and perfectly finished His task.

3. The *exaltation* of Christ (1:4). Though angels held high position in the administration of affairs in the universe, yet that One who made the world, entered the world, and redeemed the world, demonstrated by His work that He was superior to angels in nature, position, and worth, and therefore to Him was given the position of sovereign and the name which belongs to the sovereign.

II.   THE POSITION OF CHRIST AS GOD (1:5-14).

In four movements the argument supports the conclusion of the first four verses, namely, that Christ is God.

1. His relationship to the *Father* declares that He is God (vv. 5-6). From three Old Testament passages the writer proves that Christ is God (Psa. 2:7; 97:7; II Sam. 7:14). The Father declares Christ is His Son (Ps. 2:7). He demonstrates that He is His Son by resurrection (Ps. 2:7; cf. Acts 13:33). He continues in this relationship as Son (II Sam. 7:14). At the second coming He will make a revelation that He is His Son. And He will demand that adoration be paid to His Son (Ps. 97:7). Nothing like this is ever said of angels, for they are creatures and not God.

2. His relationship to the *throne* demonstrates that He is God (vv. 7-9). Angels are ministers and their only relation to the throne is to carry out its bidding. But the One who sits upon the throne is God. This throne is eternal, for ever and ever (Ps. 45:6-7). The administration of this throne is moral, for the One who sits upon it exercises a "sceptre of righteousness," that is, rightness of straightness, no crookedness or delay in justice.

3. His relationship to *creation* is further evidence that He is God (vv. 10-12). This is set forth in the three tenses of creation: past, present, and future (cf. Ps. 102:26-28).

In the *past* Christ is set forth as preexistent to, and the creator of, the universe (v. 10). At the time everything came into existence Christ already was (Gen. 1:1; cf. John 1:1, 3), and He was the One who created everything. He laid the foundation of the earth, and the heavens too are His work.

In the *present* Christ is surviving all the changes that are taking place in creation (v. 11). Created things are growing old and changing form, and are being exchanged for other things. But while all this is going on in creation, Christ, the Creator, continues right on through every change of creation without any change in Him (cf. Heb. 13:8).

In the *future* Christ will never cease to exist (v. 12). Though the things which belong to creation will change form like a vesture which is folded up, this will never be true of Christ. His years will never leave off or run out. He will remain unchangeable, being the eternal God.

4. His relationship to *authority* is final proof that He is God (vv. 13-14). He is to sit on the right hand, the place of power and authority; all enemies will be placed under His feet. But angels will serve the saints (cf. Ps. 110:1).

QUESTIONS FOR DISCUSSION

1. What place does the Epistle to the Hebrews occupy in the New Testament Canon of Scripture, and to what group of people was it written?

2. What problem faced this group of people, and what plan does the writer devise to solve this problem?

3. What relation do the first four verses of the epistle have to the rest of the book? Explain this in your own words.

4. What two periods of revelation are referred to in the first two verses of the epistle, and how do these two revelations differ?

5. What threefold perfection of Christ is discussed in relation to the universe in verses 2 and 3, and what single provision did He make for the universe?

6. What four relationships of Christ demonstrate conclusively that in position Christ is none other than God according to verses 5-14?

2

Jesus as God – Jesus as Man

The second chapter of Hebrews deals with three things. In the first four verses the writer applies what he has already taught concerning Christ in chapter 1. In verses 5-9 he points out what Christ accomplished through His humiliation. And in verses 10-18 the various arguments for the incarnation are set forth.

I. THE APPLICATION OF THE REVELATION IN CHRIST (2:1-4)

Though in former times God spoke in many portions and various ways to the fathers by the prophets, He spoke once and for all in His Son. And this revelation in His Son is perfect, infallible, complete, and final. His relationship to the Father, the throne, the creation, and authority makes it clear that Christ is God's last word to man. Without allowing the reader any room to form his own conclusions, the writer now applies this truth.

1. The *importance* of the message in Christ is set forth in verse 1. The picture in this verse is of men floating down the stream of life. From the center of the stream one can see landing places along the shore. But the current is carrying the boat along. At last there remains one more landing spot, before the dangerous rapids are reached. Once past that place there is no more hope. Only certain death awaits. So our text should read, "Therefore, it is necessary for us to give more earnest heed to the things which we have heard, lest at any time we flow on by." Christ is God's last landing spot. If men refuse to pull in and tie up to Him, nothing but the rapids and the rocks and despair are ahead.

2. The *authority* of this message is set forth by comparison with the Old Testament message (vv. 2-3). The angels carried the Old Testament Law to men (Deut. 33:2; Gal. 3:19). And it was demonstrated upon every occasion of its

infraction, that it was steadfast, inviolable, inflexible. For when it was transgressed or disobeyed it was vindicated, that is, a penalty had to be paid. And this penalty was just, and was pay back in kind, such as an eye for an eye, and a tooth for a tooth, and a life for a life (Exod. 21:23-25). If this is true of a message which God sent through angels and prophets, how much more important is the message which God sent in His Son and which is His Son. "How shall we escape, if we neglect so great salvation?"

3. The *messengers* of this message make it all the more important (v. 3). At the first this began to be spoken by Christ himself. God could not entrust this precious truth to anyone else. In fact, this message was Christ himself. He is all the truth there is about God, for He is God. But after He had spoken through His own life and ministry and went back to glory, the message was confirmed by those who witnessed His words and works, and they testified to all that He did and taught (Acts 1:1).

4. The *attestation* of this message was given by God through His servants (v. 4). In those early years God bore continuous testimony to the message spoken by the early church: by signs pointing to the meaning of things; by wonders which created amazement in the people; by miracles that could only be produced by supernatural power. Best of all, the gifts of the Holy Ghost in men and women, producing changed lives, made it clear that this is God's final message.

II. THE ACCOMPLISHMENTS OF THE HUMILIATION (2:5-9).

Now that the truth concerning the deity of Christ has been applied (2:1-4), the writer goes on with his discourse. In chapter 1 he pointed out the position of Christ in revelation.

But now he points to the position of Christ in humiliation. He is now made a little while lower than the angels (v. 9). "What," we ask, "is to be accomplished by the Son of God coming down from His regal throne and being made a little while lower than the angels?" And the answer is: "everything," so far as salvation for men is concerned. Had He brought only a message from heaven and made no provision for the realization of that message in men, He might just as well have sent the angels with the message. It was in the interest of the grand scope and plan for man that He came.

1. The proposition asserting the *final supremacy* of man is first declared (v. 5). "For unto the angels hath he not put in subjection the world to come." "The world to come" is a technical phrase pointing to the millennial kingdom. In the beginning it was in the plan of God to set man over the works of His hands (Gen. 1:27-30). But because of sin, that has been delayed. Yet God still plans to accomplish this, not now through the first Adam but through the Last Adam. Though angels are great, final supremacy will not be theirs. It is reserved for saved men who will some day rule and reign with Christ (Dan. 2:44; 7:14, 18, 27; Rev. 20:4).

2. The *purpose* setting forth final supremacy of man was revealed to the Psalmist (vv. 6-8). By rhetorical questions, the answers to which are self-evident, the Psalmist testifies to this truth (Ps. 8:4-6). What is man or the son of man? If God is mindful of him and visits him, it is because he is greater than all other created things. He has some high purpose for him. Though he is lower than the angels, it is only for a little while. In the plan of God he was crowned with glory and honor and placed over the works of His hands, and all things have been placed under his feet. And there is nothing that has not been placed under his feet. But when the Psalmist looks

again at the reality, he sees that nothing in this purpose of God has been accomplished (v. 8).

3. The *pledge* of the final supremacy of man is then declared by the writer of Hebrews (v. 9). And this pledge is in Christ. The writer of Hebrews realizes by the Spirit that the Psalmist saw the plan of God and its accomplishment. But the method by which it was to be accomplished was not revealed to him. In God's final message to men it was revealed that this high purpose was to be accomplished through Christ.

Christ *became* man and thus He too "was made a little while lower than the angels." This was humiliation for Him. For He is God, and had to step down from the high position which was rightfully His that He might be made in the likeness of men.

Only as a man could He suffer death. God is spirit and cannot die, so it was necessary that He become man in order to suffer death. In condition as man He tasted death for every man. This means that He experienced death to the full to satisfy the law's just demands and to redeem men from their fallen estate.

Because He accomplished through death this feat, He is *now crowned with glory and honor.* And His presence in heaven is the pledge that believers in Christ will be raised up with Him.

III. THE ARGUMENTS FOR THE INCARNATION OF CHRIST (2:10-18).

Though the writer of Hebrews has convincingly pointed out how sinning men are raised to the place of final supremacy through Christ, yet the necessary arguments for the humiliation of Christ by incarnation have not yet been stated. These follow immediately, and they are three in number.

1. Because of the *nature* of God it was necessary for Christ to be made perfect through suffering (vv. 10-13).

Because God's nature is what it is, it became Him, or was fitting, that He save through suffering. God is holiness, but He is also love. And in order to bring many sons into glory, the Captain, His own Son, He lovingly subjected to suffering in order that coming to perfection He might lead many sons in triumph through the gates into glory (v. 10).

But both Christ the sanctifier and they who are sanctified have the same source (v. 11). By creation Adam's race and the Last Adam come from God (Luke 3:23, 38). And by the new creation both are conceived by the Holy Spirit (Luke 1:35; John 3:5). Therefore Christ takes pride in His brethren (v. 11), and He makes a proclamation in the midst of the church of the name and praise of God for what He has done (v. 12). In this final word there is a pledge that Christ will have children to lead into glory. They are already His (v. 13).

2. Because of the *nature of men* it was necessary for Christ to become incarnated in human flesh (vv. 14-15).

In order to *destroy the devil* it was necessary to become man (v. 14). The children whom the Lord had given Him were flesh and blood. And in that realm the devil was operating. So He took the same, sin apart, and suffered death. His death was a complete satisfaction of the law. And thus Satan was robbed of all his power to longer demand death as the penalty for sin.

In order to *deliver from bondage to law* it was necessary to become flesh and die (v. 15). The strict demand of the law was absolute perfection under penalty of death. Failure put fear into human hearts. And fear forced into stricter servitude to the law. And stricter servitude brought greater infringement. And so the vicious circle went on. But Christ's death satisfied to the full the holy demands of the law and released the worshiper from this bondage.

3. Because of the *nature of the task* in saving men Christ became man (vv. 16-18).

While the work of Christ in some way affects all creation, yet *for men alone* salvation has been provided. In the realm where sin has been experienced, salvation must also be effected. That is the reason Christ took upon Him the nature of men and not angels (v. 16).

The high priest must *understand* the people for whom he intercedes. But in order to do this he must enter into the same experiences. It was therefore necessary for Christ to take upon himself human flesh and go through the experiences of temptation and suffering (vv. 17-18). He felt these things to the full, for He never fell before them into sin, and so He is completely equipped to be merciful and faithful and understanding in His high-priestly ministry (v. 18).

QUESTIONS FOR DISCUSSION

1. What is the purpose of the first four verses of chapter 2 in relation to the message of chapter 1?

2. What four things does the writer point out in this passage of Scripture that accomplish this purpose?

3. Progressing from the position of Christ in revelation, as set forth in chapter 1, to what further truth does the writer move in verses 5-9 of chapter 2?

4. How does the writer relate the purpose that God had for mankind at the beginning with the person and work of Christ?

5. In view of what the nature of God is, why was it necessary for Christ to become man according to verses 10-13?

3

From God — to the People

Our study up to the present has dealt with the position of Christ in revelation (chap. 1), and the position of Christ in redemption (chap. 2). These two ideas are now to be joined in chapters 3 and 4, for Christ's position in reconciliation is the joining of these two functions. The key is therefore at the very outset of chapter 3, "Wherefore . . . consider the Apostle and High Priest of our profession" (3:1). As the apostle or prophet of God, like Moses, He presents the revelation of God and represents God to men (chap. 3). As the High Priest for men, like Joshua, He provides rest from God and leads men to God (chap. 4). By His bringing God to men, and men to God, we see Christ's position in reconciliation (chap. 3–4). He is thus the one great mediator between God and men (Gal. 3:20; I Tim. 2:5).

In this study we shall be concentrating on chapter 3, which is occupied with the apostleship of Christ in His function of representing God to men. And throughout this chapter the final contract is thrown into contrast with the former contract. Christ is the great prophet of the final administration, while Moses is the great prophet of the former. Many in Israel failed in their response to the message of God through Moses. And many will fail in the church if they follow in the footsteps of those who failed in Israel.

I. THE FORMER COVENANT AND THE FAILURE OF SOME (3:1-11).

The great explanation by way of comparison and contrast between Christ and Moses (vv. 1-6) is followed by exhortation based upon the failure of those in Israel (vv. 7-11).

1. The *explanation* in comparison and contrast (vv. 1-6).

By *comparison* it is evident that Christ and Moses were both appointed to their task (v. 2), both were faithful in performing their task (v. 2), and both brought a message to their people (vv. 1, 5).

By *contrast* it is evident Christ is the builder of the house for He is God (vv. 3-4), while Moses was a part of the house (v. 3). Christ is a son over the house, while Moses is just a servant in the house (vv. 5-6). And since the above things are true, Christ deserves more glory than Moses (v. 3).

The *character* of the house in this passage is quite obviously the people of God in the two covenants. In the former covenant it was Israel, but in this present age it is the true Church, those who have made profession of faith in Christ, who are holy in standing, and heavenly in calling (3:1). To determine who belong in reality to this house, he asserts in verse 6 that they are those who hold fast the confidence in faith and the rejoicing of the hope firm to the end.

2. The *exhortation* based upon the failure of Israel (vv. 7-11).

The *responsibility* of the fathers in Israel is described by a quotation from the Psalms (Ps. 95:7-11) and it is used here as an appeal to the Hebrew Christians (vv. 7-9). The *time* to respond to the message from God is today (v. 7). The *method* of response is twofold: intellectually, one should hear and understand, and morally, one should not harden the heart against, but make a decision in favor of the message (vv. 7-8). The *aids* to a proper response were the trial and suffering in the wilderness (v. 8; cf. James 1:3), and God's works which were the proof of His love and care (v. 9). But *the way* Israel did respond was with bitterness (provocation) (v. 8), and the tempting of God (v. 9).

The *reaction* on the part of God toward Israel is described by the writer, and in this description there is further appeal (vv. 10-11). God was *emotionally distressed* with their actions, being "grieved with that generation" (v. 10). And He *carefully diagnosed* the condition of that people (v. 10).

Morally, "they do always err in their heart"; and intellectual-ly, "they have not known my ways." So God *justly de-stroyed* them in the wilderness (v. 11). In His wrath, a righ-teous indignation against sin, He determined to bring upon them the just penalty for their deeds. Since they refused to recognize His prophet and respond to His message, then it was only right that they should be refused the privilege of entering into His rest. By reference to the Old Testament it is evident that this great host of unbelieving Israelites never entered into the land of Canaan where there was to be ceas-ing from troubles with the nations through which they were passing.

II. THE FINAL COVENANT AND THE FAILURE OF SOME (3:12-19).

All that has hitherto preceded in this chapter is in order to further application to the Hebrew Christians who are so perilously near the same failure as their fathers of long ago. Though the fathers had sufficient light in the message from God through Moses, and were therefore guilty, deliber-ately guilty of apostasy from God, yet these Hebrew Chris-tians will be doubly guilty of apostasy if they reject the message in and through the Apostle of God, Christ Jesus the Lord. For whereas "Moses verily was faithful in all his house, as a servant, for a testimony of those things which were to be spoken after" (v. 5), and he came declaring to Israel the identity of Jehovah, "I AM THAT I AM" (Exod. 3:14); above and beyond this Christ came and declared to the people, "I am the bread of life" (John 6:35), "I am the light of the world" (John 8:12), "I am the door" (John 10:9), "I am the good shepherd" (John 10:11), "I am the resurrection, and the life" (John 11:25), "I am the way, the truth, and the life" (John 14:6), and "I am the true vine" (John 15:1). As you can see, Moses gave testimony to things yet to be spoken, while Christ is the thing spoken.

It is therefore in order to solemnly warn these Christian brethren lest they fall into the same example of unbelief. With earnest exhortation (vv. 12–15), followed by solemn explanation (vv. 16-19), the chapter proceeds.

1. The *exhortation* to avoid the failure of the past (vv. 12-15). The writer clearly describes this failure as "departing from the living God" (v. 12). The word "departing" in the original is the word "apostasy." And to escape apostasy the following things are necessary:

The *root-sin* is the evil heart of unbelief (v. 12). Since this is possible at any time, it is therefore imperative that God's people be constantly on the alert lest this sin creep up on them and steal them away from the living God.

The *method* by which this is accomplished is "through the deceitfulness of sin" (v. 13). So subtle, so seducing, so simple, and so innocent does sin appear that it plays a trick upon the moral and spiritual senses, and those who often are calculated to be the strong and spiritual are the ones who fall before its unassuming attack. For this reason it is necessary that believers exhort and encourage one another, and do so while it is called today. Yesterday is gone, and tomorrow may never come. But in the providence of God He has given us today.

The *issue* from unbelief is hardness of heart (vv. 13, 15). When unbelief continues in the life it produces a gradual hardening of the heart, so that it becomes cold and implacable and insensitive to sin. It is this gradual change in the life that fits one for hell. Once one has become confirmed in unbelief, he is beyond the reach of God's grace and in due time the sentence of God will be inflicted upon him.

The *evidence* of right relationship with Christ is persistence in faith (v. 14). If one has actually become a partaker of the nature of Christ, and is therefore truly born of God, he will give proof of this by persisting in faith with steadfastness to the very end of life. For believers then and now this point is important. Genuine Christian life is demonstrated by the continuous exercise of true Christian faith.

The *responsibility,* then, is immediate, and this means that believers should act today (v. 15). If they desire to hear the voice of the Lord, then they should not harden the heart. For hearing the voice of the Lord is more than the physical act of hearing. It involves a condition of the heart. And if the heart is not sensitive and tender the spiritual accents of His voice will never be discerned.

2. The *explanation* again comes out of the failures of the past (vv. 16-19). This incident takes the readers back to Kadesh-Barnea where the people turned back because of unbelief.

The *provocation* of unbelief was the thing that sent the people wandering for thirty-eight more years in the wilderness (v. 16). When they had come up to the very border of the Promised Land they might have entered in. But instead they chose to receive the report of ten spies rather than that of Caleb and Joshua (Num. 13:30—14:6).

The *persistence* in unbelief for forty long years produced careers of sin, which inevitably follow in the wake of sin (v. 17). Once they turned around in their hearts, there was nothing to prevent the feet from walking in the way which led back to Egypt with all of its sin and bondage.

Punishment fell upon the unbelieving multitudes during those long wilderness wanderings, just as the Lord promised (v. 17; cf. Num. 26:64-65). Of all those fighting men who were numbered by Moses and Aaron at Sinai, only two remained to enter into the Promised Land, Caleb and Joshua, who refused to turn back.

This was the direct result of the *promise* which the Lord made to the people when they turned back in unbelief (v. 18; cf. Deut. 1:34-35). It was not mere accident that Caleb and Joshua were preserved and the others perished. It was judgment upon unbelief for some and divine preservation for Caleb and Joshua.

The *conclusion* is the most mournful tale of all (v. 19). Unbelief meant that they could not enter into rest. Trials, troubles, temptation, testing, travail, turmoil, and tempest was their lot in place of the tranquillity they might have enjoyed by faith.

QUESTIONS FOR DISCUSSION

1. How is the message concerning Christ in chapters 1 and 2 now combined in the message of chapters 3 and 4? What is the key verse to chapters 3 and 4?

2. What explanation of Christ and Moses, in comparison and contrast, is made in verses 1-6?

3. How does the writer of Hebrews use the failure of some in Israel to respond rightly to the revelation through Moses as a basis to exhort Christians?

4. Verses 12-19 are further exhortation to Hebrew Christians. In what respect is the revelation in Christ even more important than that which came through Moses?

5. The writer of Hebrews describes the reaction of some in the wilderness as apostasy. Of what three things does apostasy consist as set forth in verses 12, 13, and 15?

6. Whose carcases fell in the wilderness? Name the two who entered into the land? What was the sin that was committed by those who never entered into the land?

4

Rest . . .
Past - Present -
Future

In the previous chapter we dealt with that aspect of reconciliation in which Christ, as the Apostle, brought the final and authoritative message from God in His own person. In a very real sense He represented God to men. Now, in this chapter, we are to study the other aspect of reconciliation in which Christ, as the Great High Priest, brings sinning and perishing humanity to God in His own person. As the word "Apostle" (3:1) was the key to the previous study, and Moses (3:2) the great type, so in this chapter "High Priest" (3:1; 4:14) is the key, and Joshua is the type (4:8, ASV).

Just as Moses led the people out of bondage but was unable to lead them into the land, so Joshua led them into the land but was unable to give them rest. Therefore, it is necessary to present One who not only can lead out of bondage and into the land, but also can give rest. And this is true of the great High Priest, our Lord and Saviour, Jesus Christ. The contrast is clearly this. Neither Moses nor Joshua was able to finish his task. But not so with the Lord Jesus Christ (4:10).

Since the word "rest" appears several times in chapters 3 and 4, it might be well to notice that several things are being discussed. There is, first, *creation-rest* which was accomplished by God when He finished creation (Gen. 1:31—2:3) and is memorialized by the weekly Sabbath (4:4); second, *Canaan-rest,* which was intended to be rest from the enemies of Israel and wanderings in the wilderness (3:11, 18-19; Deut. 12:9-12; Joshua 22:4), and also spiritual rest, into which Joshua was unable to lead the people (4:8); and third, *Christ's rest,* which was accomplished by Christ when He finished His work (4:10) and consists of salvation for everyone who believes in Him (4:1, 3, 5, 8-11). Christ's rest is the main topic for discussion in this chapter.

I. THE DIVINE PURPOSE OF ENTERING INTO SAL- VATION-REST STILL REMAINS (4:1-10).

God has one great purpose that is running its course through the ages and He will accomplish that purpose no matter how many obstacles appear to impede His progress or prevent Him from reaching His objective. Though Israel never entered into the rest which God offered, the purpose remains the same.

1. The *eternal promise* of entering into rest still remains (vv. 1-2). Though the writer begins an exhortation or warning to the people in the words, "Let us therefore fear, lest," he does not go on with it here, but waits until he reaches verse 11. In verses 1 through 10 he lays the foundation for what he intends to say later. But very clearly he insists that the prom- ise of entering in still remains to the people of God, and the only reason that any may seem to come short of it will be the lack of faith. For the gospel of rest has been preached to these Hebrew Christians just as it was to the Israelites of long ago, and the reason Israel did not enter into rest was unbelief (v. 2).

2. The *divine pledge* to men that a rest still remains is in the record of creation (vv. 3-5). Those who are believing are entering into rest (v. 3), and those who remain in unbelief God has sworn shall not enter into rest (v. 3). Nevertheless, when God finished His work at the time of creation every- thing was finished (v. 3), and in that fact there is the pledge that salvation-rest will be provided for all who believe (v. 4). And in this pledge there is also the solemn warning that those who do not believe shall not enter into rest (v. 5). It is evident that at the time of creation God foresaw the entrance of sin and the necessity for providing a Saviour, and in the fullness of time all this was provided in Christ (v. 10).

3. The *historic plan* for accomplishing this purpose is now stated by the writer (vv. 6-8). God's first move was to offer this rest to the people of Israel, and He therefore had the gospel of salvation-rest preached to them (v. 6). They did not enter in because of unbelief (v. 6). But God's purpose shall not fail, so it still remains that some must enter in (v. 6). So, many centuries later, "Again, he limiteth a certain day, saying in David, To day, after so long a time; as it is said, To day if ye will hear his voice, harden not your hearts" (v. 7; cf. Ps. 95:7). So in that Joshua failed to lead the people into rest (v. 8), God has made the offer again in David, and in the prophecy of David there is all that is offered to believers in this present age.

4. The *great provision* finally becomes a reality in the person and work of Christ (vv. 9-10). "There remaineth therefore a rest to the people of God" (v. 9), because "he that is entered into his rest, he also hath ceased from his own works, as God did from his" (v. 10). There was a day when Christ said, "My Father worketh hitherto, and I work" (John 5:17). And because of sin He had to keep on working. But one day He finished His task and cried out, "It is finished" (John 19:30). And then He entered into His rest. The work is done; salvation has been provided; and now into this accomplished rest He can lead everyone who believes. There remaineth therefore a rest to the people of God.

II. THE HUMAN RESPONSIBILITY OF ENTERING INTO SALVATION-REST (4:11-13).

In these verses the writer is endeavoring to drive home the personal responsibility resting upon each Christian to exercise faith in Christ as God's last word to man. He has not lost sight of the original theme expressed at the outset of the book (1:2), and at the outset of this chapter (4:2). And for the purpose of encouraging them he insists on human diligence (v. 11), points to the operation of the Word (v. 12), and describes the issue in public exposure (v. 13).

1. The *human diligence* toward the Word of God to avoid disobedience (v. 11). Whether we read "let us labour," as in the Authorized Version, or "be diligent," as in the New American Standard Bible, the meaning is simply this, that there must be active exertion to secure what God has promised. But this exertion is very clearly the exercise of the will in faith. For the writer goes on to say, "lest any man fall after the same example of unbelief." What he means is this, lest any man fall or perish, and thus provide another example, like the Israelites, of those who deliberately refuse to believe.

2. The *divine operation* of the Word of God is both encouragement and warning (v. 12). For the Word of God is able, quick, or living, like God (3:12); efficient or powerful like a two-edged sword, piercing even to the dividing of soul and spirit; and is a discerner or a judge over the feelings and thoughts of the heart. The Word is therefore able and efficient to penetrate and judge the innermost movements of soul and spirit.

3. The *ultimate issue* is public exposure before God with whom we have to do (v. 13). The spiritual technique of the Word described in verse 12 is so vital, accurate, penetrating, and thorough, everything is manifest before God. The human heart is stripped naked, no longer being able to hide behind any disguise, and what is more, like a wrestler who forces the neck of his opponent back until he is laid prostrate and defeated before the referee, so the Word of God does with a human soul who must give an account to God. It is therefore important not to trifle with the Word.

III. THE HiGH PRiEST WHO PROVIDES HELP TO ENTER INTO REST (4:14-16).

The writer has demonstrated up to this point in his discussion the superiority of Christ to angels, Moses, and Joshua. And he is now ready to set forth His superiority in priesthood. He first presents the great High Priest (v. 14), and then declares His value (vv. 15-16).

1. The *presentation* of the great High Priest (v. 14). This involves *possession,* for he says, "Seeing then that we have a great high priest." In this he is referring back to 2:17-18 and 3:1. The *provision* of the priest is also declared, "that is passed into the heavens." This means that He performed completely and perfectly the necessary work of expiation and atonement in order that He might pass through the heavens to the place of priestly ministry. The *person* of the priest is finally stated, "Jesus the Son of God." His humanity is declared in the name "Jesus" by which He was known to men, and His deity is set forth in the phrase "Son of God," which must be interpreted by all that has gone before in the letter. He is "the Son of God," through whom He utters His final speech to men.

This puts believers in a place of *responsibility*: "let us hold fast our profession" or "confession" as the original means. A profession may be a testimony offered merely among friends, but a confession, as this means, is a testimony declared in the face of opposition, which, in the light of the above facts, is the obligation of every believer.

2. The *preciousness* of the great High Priest (v. 15). The value of this priest is stated both negatively and positively. *Negatively,* "we have not an high priest which cannot be touched with the feeling of our infirmities." By "infirmities" the writer does not mean circumstances of pain, sorrow or

difficulty. An infirmity is not a material or a moral disability. It is a vulnerable point along which the enemy approaches the soul of man. The essential infirmities of humanity were exposed to view in the temptation in the wilderness, the physical relating to the body, the psychical relating to the soul, and the spiritual relating to the spirit (Matt. 4:1-11).

Positively, He "was in all points tempted like as we are, yet without sin." It is better to leave out the word "yet" which is not in the original and read it, "sin apart." It thus means that Jesus not only did not yield to temptation, but even more than that there was nothing of sin in His nature to which the enemy could appeal. This does not mean that He did not feel the force of temptation. It rather means that He felt its full force, as no other person has ever felt it. He is therefore perfectly qualified to succour those in temptation. It is therefore the believer's *responsibility* to come to the throne of grace for help (v. 16).

QUESTIONS FOR DISCUSSION

1. What are the key words and the key types to chapters 3 and 4, and what three kinds of rest are referred to in these two chapters?

2. What is God's main purpose through the ages for lost men? Does the failure in Israel change that purpose?

3. What great pledge stands as an encouragement that the promise of entering into rest still remains? What verse in this chapter cited from Psalms speaks of this?

4. In what sense does the writer of Hebrews call for the exercise of human responsibility? Is this to be confused with works?

5. What encouragement and warning does the writer cite in calling the Hebrew Christians to responsibility?

5

The High Priest and the Believer's Needs

The position of Christ in revelation (chap. 1), in redemption (chap. 2), and in reconciliation (chaps. 3–4), have been set forth. His position as God's prophet makes Him God's final word to men. His position as man's priest makes Him man's final word with God. And these two functions operating in one person make Him the perfect mediator between God and men. But to this point the writer now turns. In chapters 5–7 he will show that there is absolutely nothing lacking in Christ in His person and office as the great High Priest of the people of God. In chapter 5 the writer will discuss the qualifications of priesthood and show how they are completely possessed by Christ. In chapter 6 will follow the confirmation of His priesthood. And in chapter 7 the great illustration in Melchizedek will be set forth. So the key to this section is the word "perfect" (5:9; 6:1; 7:11).

Chapter 5 is a discussion of the qualifications of priesthood and Christ's superiority over all other priests. In the unfolding of the chapter there is first a presentation of the qualifications of priesthood (vv. 1-4), followed by the possession of these in Christ (vv. 5-10), and concluding with the perilousness of the condition of the Hebrew Christians (vv. 11-14).

I. THE PRESENTATION OF THE QUALIFICATIONS OF PRIESTHOOD (5:1-4).

The ministry of the priest is set forth in verses 1 and 2 and does not primarily have to do with qualifications. But it may be seen by looking at the work he must perform what qualifications are necessary. Fundamentally, the qualifications for priesthood have to do with person and authority (vv. 2-4).

1. The *ministry* of the priest (vv. 1-2). The *purpose* of his work is to shield men. Such is the meaning of the

phrase "for men." The *realm* of his service is "things pertaining to God," namely, that of representing them to God. The *occasion* for his work is sin and the sinfulness of men as set forth in the phrase, "for sins." Were it not for this his ministry would be unnecessary. The *material* with which he works consists of "both gifts and sacrifices," tokens of worship and atonement. The *objects* for whom he did such service are described as the "ignorant" and "them that are out of the way." The source of their sin may be ignorance, with the issue in erring, or it may mean those whose sin is predominately from ignorance, while with others it is largely wandering. Presumptuous or willful sin is not under consideration (Num. 15:22-31; Heb. 10:26ff.).

2. The *person* of the priest (vv. 2-3). Now the first qualification comes into view, namely, the capacity of the priest to sympathize with the person whom he is representing to God. The priest must therefore possess *human nature,* that is, he must be "taken from among men" (v. 1). This gives him a community of nature with those whom he serves, and enables him to understand them. But along with this, and even more important, he must experience *human need,* that is, be able to "have compassion," "for that he himself also is compassed with infirmity" (v. 2). This does not mean that he needs to have sinned, but he needs to know by experience the avenues along which sin and temptation besiege the human soul. Being clothed with such infirmity, he will have the necessary capacity to "bear gently" with his people, being neither too severe nor too lenient.

But *we should be careful* not to construe verse 3 to mean that sin is a necessary prerequisite for compassion. While in human priests, infirmity opened the way to sin, and therefore every priest had to offer first for his own sins before offering for the people. Yet by that offering there was revealed the impossibility of perfect exercise of this function on behalf of others. For to the extent of sin, to that same extent the priest is made insensitive to the weakness and sin of others. At this very point the superiority of Christ is revealed.

3. The *authority* of the priest (v. 4). We are now confronted with the second qualification for priesthood. The first was the capacity for sympathy. The second is the calling into service. For "no man taketh this honour unto himself, but he that is called of God, as was Aaron." This means that this important ministry can be performed only by one who is divinely appointed.

II. THE POSSESSION OF THE QUALIFICATIONS BY THE GREAT HIGH PRIEST (5:5-10).

In application of the above teaching to Christ you will note that the order is reversed. The writer first declares that Christ is appointed to His priesthood by God, and then he discusses capacity for sympathy. A discussion of His ministry concludes the argument.

1. The *authority* of Christ as priest (vv. 5-6). The *negative* declaration in support of this point is, "Christ glorified not himself to be made an high priest" (v. 5). The *positive* declaration is made by quotation from two Psalms (Psa. 2:7; 110:4).

From the Psalm of the Kingship of Messiah he quotes, "Thou art my Son, to day have I begotten thee." From the Psalm of the Priesthood of Messiah he quotes, "Thou art a priest for ever after the order of Melchisedec." In the first, Messiah is presented as the anointed and crowned king, while in the second, 'the essential and eternal Sonship is declared. Thus our great High Priest is both king and priest, which is precisely the connection of the name Melchisedec (or Melchizedek—cf. Gen. 14:18-20). So Christ holds the office by divine appointment.

2. The *person* of Christ as priest (vv. 7-8). The capacity for sympathy is vitally associated with the person of Christ, and as presented earlier in the chapter, this consists of two things: the possession of human nature and the experiencing of human need.

That Christ possessed *human nature,* and still does, is evident by the words "who in the days of his flesh" (v. 7). Those were the days when He lived in natural, but sinless and unglorified flesh. He lived, learned, suffered, cried, prayed, and gave way to tears like the man He was (v. 8). This placed Him in a position to understand His people.

That Christ experienced *human need* is evident from the prayer He prayed in Gethsemane (v. 7), and it was this experience which provided Him with capacity to sympathize with His people. In this verse is revealed in a new way the wonder and glory of that solemn and sublime experience in the garden. But His prayer was not that He should be saved "from" death, as some of the versions read, but "out of" death. He was going to death deliberately, by the determinate counsel and foreknowledge of God (Acts 2:23). And therefore any interpretation that suggests that He hesitated, trembled, or desired not to die is entirely unwarranted. His prayer was not that He might escape death, but that He might be saved through death, that is, out of death. In other words, His prayer was for resurrection. And He "was heard in that he feared." But it was not His fear of dying, but fear for death. Death to Him was the supreme and overwhelming tragedy of sin. Death for man was contrary to the original divine purpose. Death came in through sin, and as the sinless Man was approaching it, He faced it with horror, and cried out for deliverance out of it, for that resurrection which should be a perfect triumph over it. Nothing in all His life so completely demonstrated His ability to sympathize.

3. The *ministry* of Christ as priest (vv. 9-10). His work is now in order for discussion, since His official appointment has been declared (vv. 5-6), and His personal experience has been explained (vv. 7-8). It is these two things that brought Him to perfection as a priest.

He is therefore the *producer* of eternal salvation (v. 9). That is what the word "author" means. It is in His power to provide everything that is needed to bring His people to the place of perfection and maintain them in that position.

And His ministry is *permanent* (v. 10). For He is a priest "for ever" (v. 6), that is, bearing right on through without any interruptions or changes. This means that He can pursue His task in behalf of each saint and bring it to perfection.

III. PERILOUSNESS OF THE CONDITION OF THE HE-BREW CHRISTIANS (5:11-14).

The writer would have gone on at this point with his discussion of Melchizedek, but he felt it necessary to say some things by way of exhortation and warning. After he has completed his application of the present truth, he will resume again the main thread of discourse (6:20—7:1). He must now point out their spiritual condition (v. 11), describe their capacity (vv. 12-13), and explain the cause (v. 14).

1. The *spiritual condition* of this people is that of dullness of hearing (v. 11). They were not always dull of hearing. The original says they have become such. Dullness, or sluggishness, or slothfulness, or slowness is a moral indifference to a message. And this condition made it difficult to interpret to them the great truth about Christ, the High Priest.

2. Their *intellectual capacity* indicates arrested development, for they are babes (vv. 12-13). When they should have been fully grown and be serving as teachers of others, they were in such a state of arrested development that they must be taught again. And it was necessary to go back and teach them the first principles, the milk of the Word, the soft portions that do not require any vigorous exercise of the mind to receive and digest.

3. The *underlying cause* is now clearly stated by the writer (v. 14). Those who are of "full age," that is, mature, have not fallen into the *sin of stagnation,* the refusal to use their senses, nor into the *sin of insensitiveness,* the refusal to see sin and depart from it. Babes have deliberately thrust aside the necessary aids to growth and maturity.

QUESTIONS FOR DISCUSSION

1. What is the key word in chapters 5-7, and in what sense is this to be understood in relation to Christ?

2. What is the movement of thought in these three chapters as related to Christ in His priesthood?

3. What is meant by the words, "for that he himself also is compassed with infirmity" (v. 2) in relation to the qualifications of the priest, and how was this fulfilled in Christ?

4. What groups of words in verses 5-10 indicate that Christ possessed human nature and experienced human need? What is the meaning of the phrase "from death" in verse 7?

5. In making the application to these Hebrew Christians, what two adverse conditions did the writer point out according to verses 11-13?

6. When uncovering the underlying cause for these conditions, to what two sins did the writer point that marked them as babes?

6

Forward March!

In masterly fashion the writer has exhibited the superiority of the priesthood of Christ over all other priests. Any failure on the part of believers to see this superiority is not because of any essential lack in the priesthood itself, nor any inability on the part of the writer to display this superiority. Any failure lies in the condition of those to whom he is writing (5:11-14).

The apparent abandonment of his theme is only temporary for the purpose of giving some much needed warning and explanation, and then he will again resume the study of Christ's priesthood. In this chapter his specific purpose is encouragement by pointing to the confirmation of the Melchizedekian priesthood (v. 16). In order to properly prepare his readers he first exhorts them to go on to perfection (vv. 1-8), then gives an explanation of their present condition (vv. 9-12), and finally points to the divine encouragement to go on (vv. 13-20).

I. THE EXHORTATION TO GO ON TO PERFECTION (6:1-8).

The argument proceeds through three movements, the writer insisting first that progress should characterize the believer's life (vv. 1-3), and second that there is peril of apostasy for every believer (vv. 4-6), and finally that productivity from life is evidence of condition (vv. 7-8).

1. *Progress* should characterize the believer's life (vv. 1-3). This is true, first of all, in the teaching which the believer receives. It must be true there, before growth can appear in the life. "Wherefore leaving the doctrine of the first principles of Christ, let us press on unto perfection" (v. 1, ASV). If anything, these Hebrew Christians were holding back. They didn't want to move on. The writer makes the appeal to them to yield, surrender, this being admirably

brought out by the original, "Let us be borne on to perfection." The power is operating; the writer is ready to move on. All he needs is the willing surrender of his audience. And he is determined to go on "if God permit" (v. 3). Apparently God did, judging from chapter 7.

But this progress in teaching, "leaving the doctrine of the first principles of Christ," does not mean that the first principles are unimportant. They are first principles, and must be left, not in the sense of denying them, but in that of recognizing them and then proceeding on to a consideration of greater truths which bring to perfection. These first principles are repentance, faith, teaching of baptisms, the laying on of hands, resurrection of the dead, and eternal judgment. All of these are taught in the Old Testament and are essentially primary truths in the early doctrinal experience of every believer. But the believer must not remain there. He must go on. If these truths bring him to Christ and he turns back, that is fatal.

2. *Peril* of apostasy is therefore something of which believers need to be warned (vv. 4-6). The writer of this booklet does not insist that he has the final word of interpretation on this passage, but he does offer what seems to him to be the easiest solution. For the sake of argument the writer of Hebrews is putting the matter on the plane of the claims made by these Hebrew Christians.

The description in verses 4 and 5 marks these as *Christian people.* They have received revelation from God (once enlightened, cf. 10:32); they have experienced redemption (tasted of the heavenly gift, John 3:16); they have been regenerated (made partakers of the Holy Ghost, John 3:5); and they have experienced the promises and realities of the future (tasted the good word of God, and the powers of the world to come, Zech. 1:13; Heb. 2:4-5).

The *supposition* is that such persons "shall fall away," which does not mean stumble, but apostatize (same word used in Septuagint, Ezek. 18:24; 20:27). This is in full accord with other passages in this epistle (Heb. 10:38-39), and especially with Hebrews 3:12 where the word apostatize is used. This is crucifying the Son of God afresh and making a public and infamous display of Him. Whatever this is, we must agree there is something ominous and terrifying about it.

The *conclusion* is this, that it is impossible to renew them to repentance. Repentance is the first of the first principles. This must mean that turning from the great salvation makes it impossible to get back. If the first repentance did not suffice, it is difficult to see how a second experience would be any more effective. Surely this Scripture has no reference either to the man who has never heard the Gospel, or to the child of God who falls by the way, and being concerned about his fall, does repent. It is for those who, having come to share in salvation, deliberately reject the mediatorial work of Christ.

3. The *productivity* of the soil is the evidence of the condition of the ground (vv. 7-8). Good ground receives blessing of rain, and produces fruit for the dresser (v. 7). But bad ground, though it receives the same rain, will produce nothing but thorns and briars, and is therefore nigh unto cursing and the end, which is to be burned (v. 8). And such is also true of human life. To this point the writer now proceeds.

II. THE EXPLANATION OF THEIR PRESENT CONDITION (6:9-12).

It will be seen in these words that the writer does not believe that any such thing can happen to a true child of God. His persuasion based upon what he has seen in their lives is sufficient to lead him to another conclusion (vv. 9-10). And what he has seen stirs within him a deep passion for their progress in the Christian life (vv. 11-12).

1. The *persuasion* based upon the fruitfulness of their lives (vv. 9-10). "Though we thus speak" is the key to the above argument (vv. 4-6). For he is persuaded better things, the things which issue forth from salvation. Worse things issue from the absence of salvation. And to apostatize would certainly be worse.

Nor is the writer doing wishful thinking. He has seen the *product* of their lives (v. 10). Their work and labor of love in ministry to the saints in the past is commendable, and the same ministry in the present is further evidence. This is not only convincing to the writer, but he insists that "God is not unrighteous to forget" these things.

2. This leads to an expression of the great *passion* he has for these Christians (vv. 11-12). It is his desire that the same diligence be exercised with full assurance of hope to the very end of their lives (v. 11). It is the continuation in the above things (v. 10) that is the full guarantee that they are Christians.

The final appeal is that they might not be sluggish as he first described them (5:11), "but followers of them who through faith and patience inherit the promises" (v. 12). They had become sluggish. But he is warning them lest they become absolutely and finally sluggish. This would be the end. And there is no better way to avoid such than to become imitators of them who through the exercise of faith go on, and in spite of hardships of the way exercise long-suffering, and in so doing inherit the promises.

III. THE ENCOURAGEMENT OF THEM TO GO ON TO PERFECTION (6:13-20).

How appropriate this final word following upon the most solemn and terrifying warning in the entire Bible. God is for every saint, as well as the writer. And in this paragraph God's infinite compassion and tenderness toward the saint is exhibited. He wants His own to "have a strong consolation," or a "strong encouragement" (v. 18), and therefore He has sworn "an oath for confirmation" (v. 16).

1. The *promise to Abraham* was confirmed with an oath and fulfilled (vv. 13-15). The promise made to Abraham is expressed in verse 14, "Surely blessing I will bless thee, and multiplying I will multiply thee." This is the central idea. Isaac was the immediate seed and Christ the ultimate. This is the promise that was ratified by an oath (v. 13; cf. Gen. 22:16). It is mentioned in Genesis 12:3, 7 and again in 15:5, and confirmed in 22:15-18. Only through long-suffering did Abraham obtain it. Twenty-five years elapsed from the call of Abraham to the birth of Isaac (cf. Gen. 12:4 with 21:5). But the birth of Isaac was only part of the promise. It was completely fulfilled in Christ who became High Priest and has entered within the veil.

2. The promise was also to the *seed of Abraham* who were his heirs (vv. 16-18). Where there are matters in dispute, an oath is the method of settling it once and for all (v. 16). This was the method used among men. An oath was the calling upon a higher power to witness to the veracity of a statement, with some severe penalty attached to guarantee the carrying out of the statement. Since the heirs of Abraham begin with Isaac (Gen. 15:4), and extend to Christ (Gal. 3:16), believers in Christ enter into the promise (Gal. 3:29). So to all these God desired to show the unchangeableness of

His counsel, and therefore confirmed His promise with an oath. And being without a greater than himself to swear by, He swore by himself (v. 13). There were then two unchangeable things, the promise and the oath, which guaranteed the fulfillment of the program outlined to Abraham and his seed, with the final culmination in the High Priesthood of Christ.

3. The promise then is *completely fulfilled* in the exalted Christ (vv. 19-20). Christ, the High Priest, is the hope set before believers (v. 18); and having entered within the veil, He is an anchor for the soul, both sure and steadfast (v. 19). The anchor is sure because it is rooted within the veil where the circumstances of a sinful world do not disturb it. It is steadfast because it is made of stuff that is firm and unyielding, a Christ who is God and Man and without sin. He is the forerunner for us, and is therefore the pledge that we too shall some day follow Him into heaven. The chief reason we have hope is that He is our great High Priest after the order of Melchizedek. His continuous and effective session at the right hand of the throne will complete the salvation He has already begun in us.

QUESTIONS FOR DISCUSSION

1. What is the main theme of chapter 6, and how is it related to the closing words of chapter 5?

2. What are the principles of the doctrine of Christ, and what is meant by leaving them to go on to perfection?

3. What is the meaning of verses 4-6? What two interpretations cannot be in the mind of the writer of the epistle?

4. If it is possible for a person to experience that thing described in verses 4-6, what is his final situation?

5. Even though the writer of Hebrews has spoken as he has in verses 4-6, what is his persuasion concerning the people to whom he is writing and why?

7

Contrasts Between Two Priesthoods

The writer has now returned to the main stream of thought, "Jesus, made an high priest for ever after the order of Melchisedec" (6:20). In chapter 5 the writer enumerated the qualifications of priesthood and demonstrated how beautifully these were possessed by Christ, our great High Priest (5:1-10). He was just ready to discuss in more detail the perfections of this priest, when the sluggishness of his audience made it necessary to deal with some matters of personal importance to them (5:11—6:19). But in the course of this discussion he has finally reached the main line once more (6:20).

Chapter 7 is a presentation of the great Melchizedekian order of priesthood with its central point resting in the perfection it is able to give. "If therefore perfection were by the Levitical priesthood, (for under it the people received the law,) what further need was there that another priest should rise after the order of Melchisedec, and not be called after the order of Aaron?" The answer to this question is self-evident, but the chapter gives a clear explanation.

The subject is developed in three movements: a consideration of the Melchizedekian priesthood (vv. 1-10); the contrast with the Levitical priesthood (vv. 11-25); and the conclusion concerning the priesthood of Christ (vv. 26-28).

I. THE CONSIDERATION OF THE MELCHIZEDEKIAN PRIESTHOOD (7:1-10).

The key word is in verse 4, "Now consider how great this man was." And this is done by giving a description of the priesthood (vv. 1-3) and then an evaluation of it (vv. 4-10).

1. The *description* of the priesthood of Melchizedek (vv. 1-3). This consists of his historical appearance (vv. 1-2), his essential significance (v. 2), and his official characteristics (v. 3).

The *historical appearance* of Melchizedek is recorded in Genesis 14:18-20 (vv. 1-2). His Hebrew name, Melchi-zedek, means king of righteousness. He was king of Salem, which is to be identified with Jerusalem (Ps. 76:2). He had a twofold position, that of king administering the affairs of state among men, and that of priest representing his people to the Most High. There is every reason to believe that this historical personage was a worshiper of the true God or else Abraham would have had no dealings with him. His twofold position provided an ideal situation, and one which looks forward to the Millennium, when our great High Priest-King will be administering the affairs of state and God. His experience with Abraham is briefly told. He met Abraham returning from the slaughter of the kings, and blessed him. And Abraham paid to him tithes of spoils he had taken from the vanquished kings.

The *essential significance* of Melchizedek is best discovered by noting the phrase "being by interpretation" (v. 2). He tells us the meaning of his name. It is "King of righteousness," and since a name refers to all that a person is, we may logically assume that this man was righteous. His position is interpreted as king of peace, which refers not to a city by that name, but the issue of this man's life and ministry. The order is divine: first, righteousness; and then peace, the fruit of righteousness (James 3:15-18).

The *official characteristics* of this man are also listed "by interpretation" (v. 3). There were no official records kept of his father or mother, for in this city-state of long ago, there was no official priestly caste or royal clan. The king-priest was elected from among the common people on the basis of personal qualifications. There were no genealogical tables (descent) of him, nor any official records of the date of his birth or death. So that the only glimpse we get of him is in office, living, serving, and never being succeeded by another. In this respect he becomes a remarkable type of the Son of God.

2. The *evaluation* of the priesthood of Melchizedek is made by comparison with Levi and Abraham (7:4-10).

It is evident that he was *greater than Abraham,* the father of Levi (vv. 4-7). Abraham recognized the fact that he was greater than he, for he paid tithes to him and was blessed by him (vv. 4, 7). And he was *greater than Levi,* for his life was longer (v. 8). Levi died, and all the priests out of his loins have also died. But this man liveth. And for that matter, his superiority over Levi was evidenced by the fact that *Levi paid tithes to him* in Abraham (vv. 9-10). That day when Abraham paid tithes to Melchizedek, Levi was yet in the loins of Abraham, and therefore in substance he recognized that he was inferior to Melchizedek.

II. THE CONTRAST BETWEEN THE LEVITICAL AND MELCHIZEDEKIAN PRIESTHOODS (7:11-25).

The general statement of difference is made in verse 11. It is a question to which the answer is self-evident. The Levitical priesthood was not able to bring anyone to perfection. It did what it could and failed because it was based upon the law and human nature (Rom. 8:3-4). But the Melchizedekian priesthood was planned to succeed it, and would accomplish the task where the former had failed. The specific reasons why the first failed and the final will succeed now follow.

1. The Melchizedekian priesthood is greater because it is a *royal priesthood* (vv. 12-14). The key words are "another tribe" (v. 13) and "Judah" (v. 14). Of this tribe nothing was ever said about priests, for the priestly tribe was Levi. So a priest from the tribe of Judah marks a difference in the external system, and here is where it differs with the Levitical

priesthood. So the Melchizedekian priesthood goes beyond the Levitical ministry at the altar and includes also the royal prerogatives of government. In this great King-Priest the two great functions of mediation meet. There is the administration of God's law over and upon man as King, and the representation of failing men to God as Priest. And best of all, mediation between God and men reaches its perfection, for God is in Christ.

2. The Melchizedekian priesthood is greater because it is an *indissoluble priesthood* (vv. 15-19). The key phrase is "an endless life" (v. 16). This phrase means the life cannot be dissolved from within, and therefore the contrast with the Levitical priesthood may be said to lie in *internal nature.* The Levitical priesthood was "after the law of a carnal commandment" (v. 16). This means that the Old Testament law prescribed certain stipulations about the flesh, such as family, bodily condition, marriage, infirmities, mortality, and such like. A man had to belong to the tribe of Levi, be without physical blemish, and when he died he had to have a successor. Since he was a man in whom the seeds of death were operating, it meant that his power to serve would sooner or later come to an end. But not so with the Lord Jesus Christ. There were no seeds of death within Him. And therefore operating under the power of such a life, His service would never end.

3. The Melchizedekian priesthood is greater because it is an *immutable priesthood* (vv. 20-22). The key to this point is in the phrase "with an oath" (v. 21; cf. Ps. 110:4). It was the oath which settled matters once and for all and forever. So this means that this priesthood stands in contrast with the Levitical in the realm of *divine plan.* The Levitical priests were not placed in office by an oath, which meant that this system was temporary, and while serving its purpose for the

time, it would pass away and be succeeded by a system that was permanent. So the former system has passed away, and the new priesthood has come upon the scene and will remain forever. The Melchizedekian priesthood is unchangeable.

4. The Melchizedekian priesthood is greater because it is an *uninterrupted priesthood* (vv. 23-25). The key to this fact is the phrase "an unchangeable priesthood" (v. 24). This does not mean the same as the former point. In the former, the entire system was in mind. But here the writer has in mind each priest in the system. It is *personal tenure in office* wherein the contrast lies with the Levitical. In that system, a priest lived out his days and died, and another had to take up his work and go on; and then he was succeeded by yet another, and so on. But in the Melchizedekian system there is just one priest who continues in office forever. This enables him to undertake a task and complete it. Or, as the writer puts it, "he is able also to save them to the uttermost." By this final word he means completely and to the very finish.

III. THE CONCLUSION CONCERNING THE PRIESTHOOD OF CHRIST (7:26-28).

With bold and beautiful strokes the writer draws the final picture of our great Melchizedekian Priest, describing His essential person, His sufficient sacrifice, and His perpetual priesthood.

1. In treating the *essential person* of Christ he gives a description of His personal qualities (v. 26). In conduct He is holy as to himself and harmless as far as others are concerned. In character He is undefiled. He could walk through a sinful world without responding to it. In condition He is set apart morally from sinners, and positionally He is far above even the intelligences of heaven.

2. In touching upon His *sufficient sacrifice* he has in mind the priestly offering of Christ (v. 27). One offering was enough, for it was sufficient in value. Not so the Levitical priests. For them it was one continual task, day after day; first, for their own sins, which showed the deficiency of the priest; and then daily for the people, which demonstrated the lack in each offering. But Christ did it just once for the people, himself excepted, never to be repeated.

3. In concluding—it is the *perpetual priesthood,* His permanent ministry, that reassures the saint (v. 28). The word of the oath established the Son in this office, and He has been perfected for His task, and therefore will bear right on through the years performing the ministry which will bring through to perfection every saint who looks to Him.

QUESTIONS FOR DISCUSSION

1. In returning to the main argument of the epistle, to what great historical person does the writer point as an illustration of Christ?

2. In what historical situation does this person appear? What facts do we learn about him from the record of Scripture?

3. What is the essential significance of this man, and what are his official characteristics? What sort of evaluation is placed upon him?

4. In setting forth the contrast with the Levitical priesthood, explain what is meant by "another tribe" (v. 13) and "Juda" (v. 14).

5. What is meant by the expression, "an unchangeable priesthood" (v. 24) in setting forth one of the characteristics of the Melchizekian priesthood of Christ?

8

The New
and the Old

The superiority of the Son has been clearly displayed in the argument of the epistle up to this point. He is superior in His position as prophet (chap. 1), as priest (chap. 2), and as mediator (chaps. 3-4). And He is also superior in priesthood, for perfection is in Him (chap. 5), its confirmation was made by oath (chap. 6), and the great illustration is Melchizedek (chap. 7). It is now time to point out the provision of Christ, that is, the superiority of the consequent relationships (chaps. 8-10). This provision consists of a better covenant (chap. 8), a new sanctuary (chap. 9), and one sacrifice (chap. 10).

In this lesson we shall study largely the better covenant in its contrast with the old covenant. But we shall divide the chapter into three sections: the first dealing with the High Priest (vv. 1-2), the second describing the heavenly ministry (vv. 3-6), and the third setting forth the better covenant (vv. 6-13).

I.   THE HIGH PRIEST—"We have such an high priest"— (8:1-2).

1. The *chief point* is now before the mind's eye of the writer, and he desires to get it before his readers. In the Amplified Version verse 1 reads, "Now of the things which we have spoken this is the *sum.*" In the American Standard Version it reads, "Now in the things which we are saying the chief point is this." He means to say that every bit of the argument up to this point has been directed to what he is about to say.

2. The *essential person* of Christ is that point. "We have such an high priest." Into the word "such" everything should be read which has been written of Him. It is not enough to consider that which has immediately preceded. One must go back to the very beginning of the book and gather up every-

thing. He is the person through whom God has spoken in revelation (chap. 1), the priest through whom man has been represented in redemption (chap. 2), the mediator by whom God and men have been brought together in reconciliation (chaps. 3-4), the one perfectly equipped to sympathize with men (chap. 5), the one officially installed by oath (chap. 6), and the one exercising a Melchizedekian priesthood (chap. 7). Everything depends upon the perfect recognition of this Priest in himself.

3. The *heavenly place* He serves is also important. It is "on the right hand of the throne of the Majesty in the heavens" (v. 1). He is there as "a minister of the sanctuary, and of the true tabernacle, which the Lord pitched, and not man" (v. 2). By this method of statement the writer draws the attention of Hebrew Christians to the fact that the things with which they had been associated in the past were not the real or the final things. By the use of the word "true" he does not imply that the earthly things were untrue. He simply means that they were shadows, copies, outlines, indeed divinely arranged, but still preparatory and transitory. Into the holy of holies in heaven our great High Priest has entered and there ministers in our behalf today.

4. The *official position* of this High Priest is indicated by the phrase "who sat down" (8:1 ASV). This is a rather remarkable statement in view of the Hebrew customs. This was never the position of the high priest as he ministered in the holy of holies. That the high priest of the Old Testament covenant always stood while ministering was indicative that his task was never complete. But our High Priest, entering in, sat down, and thus signified the absolute completion and perfection of His mediatorial ministry. This is not to be confused with that ministry to the saints, as in the case of

Stephen (when Jesus was seen standing in heaven, Acts 7:55-56). As long as God's people are passing through the hour of need, this standing ministry will never be completed.

II. THE HEAVENLY MINISTRY—"a more excellent ministry" (8:3-6).

The result of all these things in the case of the Priest himself is that He exercises a more excellent ministry (v. 6), which may be analyzed as to purpose (v. 3), location (v. 4), description (v. 5), and evaluation (v. 6).

1. The *purpose* of this ministry is to offer gifts and sacrifices (v. 3). While it is the plan of the writer to discuss in some detail this matter at a later time, his only desire at this point is to mention it in passing. As a matter of fact, it has already been revealed (1:3), and he will shortly return to it. We can say here that Christ offers himself, in all the fulness of that suggestion, in the perfection of His person, in the mystery of His atonement, and in the power of His resurrection.

2. It is the *location* of this ministry, however, to which the writer is moving (v. 4). "For if he were on earth, he should not be a priest." And this is true because the law established priests in the earth, and made no provision for the ministry of any other priest. Being of the tribe of Judah, He is thus excluded from priestly ministry in the earth. And there would be no point anyway in serving in the earth, for His priestly ministry in earth would be scarcely better than the priestly ministry He would supersede. His ministry is ordained for the skies.

3. Therefore a *description* of His ministry is in order (v. 5). But this is given by pointing to the earthly and implying the heavenly. The earthly ministry was an *imitation* while the

heavenly is *original.* Such is the meaning of the word "example." The earthly ministry was only *shadow* while the heavenly is *substance.* This is suggested by the word "shadow." And the earthly was only *outline* while the heavenly is *fulness,* this being suggested by the word "pattern." It is therefore evident that the Old Testament priest in his ministry could only point to possibilities, while our great High Priest can produce realities.

4. The *evaluation* of this ministry finally follows as a logical conclusion (v. 6). "But now hath he obtained a more excellent ministry." The words "minister" (v. 2) and "ministry" are made upon the same root and mean active in behalf of the people. When it is then realized that this minister in His ministry is active in behalf of the people, and exercises it in the true place, as a perfect priest, with the sufficient offering, it is obvious that this is a more excellent ministry, by which the writer means that it is perfect. There is nothing lacking in it which is necessary to save those to the uttermost who come to God by Him, "*seeing* He ever liveth to make intercession for them" (7:25). This leads logically to the new contractual relationship established by this Priest between God and those whom He represents.

III. THE BETTER COVENANT—"He is the mediator of a better covenant" (8:6-13).

Five ideas explain why this new covenant was a better covenant than the former. It was founded, needed, promised, described, and assured.

1. The new covenant was *founded* upon better promises and therefore it was better (v. 6). As most people know, a building is no better than its foundation. If the superstructure is to have any enduring qualities, it must be reared

upon a good foundation. And the same thing is true of the making of covenants or contracts. The first covenant was made at Sinai (v. 9) and it was between God and His people, and based upon the promises of the people (Exod. 19:5-8), while the final covenant is based solely upon the promises of God (Jer. 31:31-34).

2. The new covenant was *needed* as the failures of the people only too clearly indicated (vv. 7-8). If the first covenant had been faultless, there would have been no need for a final. But deficiency is not to be attributed to the covenant as such, nor to God, one of the contracting parties. The sole fault lay with the people of Israel. They were unable to keep their commitments, and they were unable to satisfy the righteous demands of the law which they incurred by their failure to keep the contract.

3. So the new covenant was *promised* at that time in Israel when her failure was evident (vv. 8-9). Since the first covenant had failed because there was no provision in it to deal with sinful and weak human nature, the new covenant was to be totally unlike the first. There was to be in it the necessary qualities to care for failing human nature. For what the law could not do in that it was weak through the flesh (Rom. 8:3), the new covenant would do. And in this sense this became one of the prophecies of hope during this dark day in Israel.

4. Then the new covenant is *described* for the further encouragement of these Hebrew Christians (vv. 10-12). And this description is threefold.

First, the new covenant consists in *regeneration,* being internal and not external as the old (v. 10). This time the laws are to be placed in their minds and written upon their hearts, and not written down on statute books. Mental understanding and moral inclination toward the laws of God constitute the new nature. It is the presence of the Spirit of God within.

Second, the new covenant will produce *illumination,* for it will not be didactic but intuitive (v. 11). It will not be necessary for each one to teach his neighbor, saying, "Know the Lord," for all will know Him from the least to the greatest. It is the presence of the Spirit within who teaches each man of the Lord (I John 2:20, 27).

Third, the new covenant is based upon *justification,* and thus it is gracious and not vindictive as was the old (v. 12). "For I will be merciful to their unrighteousness, and their sins and their iniquities will I remember no more." Here is the reason God could impart His own nature to men. He freed men from the penalty of sin by being gracious to them in Christ, and released himself to give them the positive blessing of His own indwelling presence.

5. The new covenant has been *assured* in its very mention (v. 13). The word "new" means in the sense of form, nature, impulse, and surety, not in the sense of years. But it also means that the old has fulfilled its purpose and must pass.

QUESTIONS FOR DISCUSSION

1. In moving to chapters 8-10, what three things as set forth in these chapters are provided by the ministry of Christ?

2. In stating that this is the "sum" (KJV) or "chief point" (ASV), to what three things, according to verses 1-2, is the writer calling attention in the priesthood of Christ?

3. Where is the ministry of Christ as a priest discharged, and why must His ministry be carried on in this place?

4. What three contrasting characteristics does the writer

point to in differentiating the heavenly ministry from the earthly ministry according to verse 5?

5. Quite specifically, what was the old covenant as referred to in verse 9, and what is the new covenant according to verse 10?

6. Why was the new covenant better than the old, as described in verses 10-12, and is the true believer today participant in the new?

9

The Heavenly

vs

the Earthly

As a result of the more excellent ministry of our great High Priest, we have now to look in upon the better worship provided in the heavenly sanctuary. Three things go to make up this better worship: a new sanctuary, a new service, and one sacrifice. The first two of these are treated in chapter 9.

I. THE EARTHLY SANCTUARY AND ITS SERVICE (9:1-10).

To alert the reader for what will follow, the writer declares in verse 1 that he intends to talk briefly about the sanctuary and service which belong to the first covenant. This is in order, for it refreshes the memory of his readers concerning the earthly things, which he will shortly remind them are but copies of the heavenly.

1. The *sanctuary and its furniture* (vv. 2-5). It is the Tabernacle in the wilderness of which he is informing them, and he is careful to point out that it had two parts.

The *first tabernacle* (v. 2), or the first part of the Tabernacle, contained three articles of furniture: the candlestick, the table of shewbread, and the golden altar of incense before the veil which guarded the holy of holies. This compartment was called the holy place.

The *second tabernacle* (vv. 3-5), or second compartment, was divided from the first by a huge veil. In it was the ark of the covenant, containing the tables of law, the pot of manna, and Aaron's rod. Resting on the ark was the mercy seat, and overshadowing the mercy seat were the cherubim of glory. The golden censer or altar of incense is mentioned here, not because it stood within the veil, but because the priest went from it within the veil (cf. Exod. 30:6 with Lev. 16:12-13).

2. The *sanctuary and its service* (vv. 6-7). In these two

verses the writer briefly describes the service in each compartment of the Tabernacle.

Into the *first tabernacle* or compartment many priests
went daily accomplishing the service of God (v. 6). But per-
formance in the holy place is not so remarkable.

Into the *second tabernacle* or compartment one priest
went, quite alone, once a year, carrying blood on his own
behalf and for the people (v. 7). Only the mystery of infinite
grace will explain how the high priest, without any inherent
right, gained admittance to the holy of holies.

3. The *significance of this service* (vv. 8-10). It should be
noted that this Old Testament Tabernacle was designed to
teach some lessons, and these lessons through the Tabernacle
are signified by the Holy Spirit.

The first is that the *way into the holiest* or second compartment was not yet made manifest, so long as the veil
separated it from the first compartment and allowed only
one priest to enter there once each year (v. 8).

The second lesson is the basis for the first, namely, that
the *worshiper* was not made perfect (v. 9). Though endless
ritual and sacrifice were made in behalf of each worshiper,
yet this never relieved any Jewish conscience of the burden
of guilt. And so long as the worshiper was not absolutely
holy, the veil dividing the first compartment from the second
could not be removed.

The third lesson is the basis for the second, that all the
works making up the service of the Jewish Tabernacle were
carnal (v. 10). This does not mean that they were sinful. It
only means that being of the flesh, they were without sufficient value, and were imposed temporarily until the time of
reformation.

So the argument is quite decisive. The works of the

Tabernacle were without sufficient value (v. 10). And since they were without necessary value the worshiper remained imperfect. And since the worshiper was imperfect, he had no right to enter into the most holy place. And since he had no right to enter into the most holy place, the way into the holiest was not made manifest. One day when that veil separating the holy from the most holy was rent from the top to the bottom, it was then manifest that this whole earthly Tabernacle had fulfilled its purpose, for then the most holy place in heaven was open to all who would place trust in Christ.

II. THE HEAVENLY SANCTUARY AND ITS SERVICE (9:11-22).

The key to this division of our study is stated in verse 11, "But Christ being come an high priest." This does not mean that He became a high priest, although He did. It rather means that He has now arrived at the place where He can perform high priestly ministry. He has entered into the most holy place in heaven where He will serve. His arrival affects three things.

1. The *sanctuary and its spiritual quality* (vv. 11-12). Into a greater and more perfect tabernacle He entered. It was so because it was not made with hands, for it was not of this creation. And His entrance there was not through symbolic blood of bulls and goats, but through His own blood which constituted His right to enter there once for all, that is, to remain, and perpetually exercise the ministry of that sacred place. He entered there by the inherent right of His own holiness, and by the acquired right of atonement to represent sinning men. When the veil of the Temple was rent in twain from top to bottom, it was thus signified that He had accomplished eternal redemption, and the distinction between

the holy and the most holy place was ended. His work of atonement was accomplished and He entered into the most holy, there to represent us before God. And never having to pass out again, He receives us, and introduces us through himself to direct and personal communion with God. His entrance there does not issue in the destruction of priesthood. It results in the constitution of the wider priesthood of all believers.

2. The *service and its sanctifying power* (vv. 13-14). At this point the writer throws into bold contrast the service performed in the sanctuaries old and new. He does admit that the old service had a cleansing power which was *ceremonial, external, effective* (v. 13). But how much more the blood of Christ. Its cleansing power was *actual*, personal, vital. It penetrated to the very moral center of man. It was therefore *internal* in its effect, for it touched the conscience. How different the offering of Christ as contrasted with that of animals. His offering was voluntary, rational, spontaneous, moral, and holy. His offering was *positive* for it produced service toward God.

3. The *surety of inheritance and its support* (vv. 15-22). Proceeding from cleansing power, he insists that the blood of Christ is a guarantee of inheritance (v. 15). It is this blood which made Christ the mediator of the new covenant. But before any positive blessings could be communicated to men, the sin problem between God and men had to be settled. And once it was dealt with the "called" were eligible for eternal inheritance. But death alone will bring the will (testament) into force (vv. 16-17), and this is because those who were once alienated must be restored to sonship. And to demonstrate the logic of his argument, the writer points out how this same thing was true of the first covenant (vv. 18-22).

III. THE ETERNAL SALVATION AND ITS SIGNIFI-CANCE (9:23-28).

The service performed by Christ is now presented in its mediatorial efficacy. The perfection of His service as priest is now set forth in its two phases. The first is that of the priest entering into the most holy place (vv. 24-26), and the second is that of the priest coming forth from the most holy place (vv. 27-28). Verse 23 is an introduction to the argument.

1. The *priest entering in* to the most holy place (vv. 24-26). It is necessary to keep in mind the tabernacle service in the wilderness to appreciate fully the sense of these verses. The great Day of Atonement is in the mind of the writer.

The *spiritual substance* of the place where Christ enters is the first point he makes (v. 24). On the great Day of Atonement the high priest entered into the place made with hands. And it was shadow, not substance. It was a figure, not the true. But not so with Christ. He entered into heaven itself now to appear in the presence of God for us. The predictive, the picturesque, the promise, is now becoming a reality.

The *single offering* made by Christ stands in contrast with the many offerings in Israel (v. 25). Once every year the high priest in Israel entered in to make atonement for the people, and he always carried the blood of others, that is, animals. But with Christ it was different. His offering was himself, and if He followed the course of Jewish priests, He would have suffered often. But it was not necessary to offer more than once.

The *sufficient sacrifice* He made forever put away sin, for it was the sacrifice of himself (v. 26). Once in the end of the age He suffered without the camp, and then made His way into heaven where He appeared with His blood to put away sin. This verse does not refer to His advent into the world, but His advent in glory when His earthly mission was accomplished. It was in heaven and before the face of God that He was manifested.

2. The *priest coming forth* from the most holy place (vv. 27-28). Again it is the tabernacle ritual before us. The people always waited outside for the issue of the priest's entrance into the most holy place on the Day of Atonement. If God received the offering, the priest would come forth as evidence that it had received the approval of God.

Since the death of men is followed by the issue of their lives (v. 27), it is expected that the death and offering of Christ in heaven will also be followed by issue. Moreover, Christ went into the holy of holies and made the offering of His blood, and sat down, which is the proof of a completed task. He will also come forth again, as did the high priest in figure, and this time He will appear to them who are looking to His offering for salvation, but apart from sin.

QUESTIONS FOR DISCUSSION

1. What three things make up the better worship of the believer under the new covenant, and what two are discussed in chapter 9?

2. How was the earthly sanctuary constructed and what furniture was to be found in the various compartments? (See vv. 2-5).

3. According to verses 6 and 7, which priests ministered in the various compartments of the earthly tabernacle?

4. According to verses 8-10, what lessons did the Holy Spirit teach in the service of the earthly tabernacle?

5. Why was the heavenly tabernacle greater and more perfect (vv. 11-12), why did its service have sanctifying power (vv. 13-14), and why did it give surety of inheritance (vv.

15-22)?

6. What does the entering into heaven on the part of Christ signify, and what does His coming forth mean, according to verses 23-28?

10

It Was Sufficient

In our study of the provision of Christ (chaps. 8-10), the writer has presented the better covenant, with the writing of the laws upon the mind and heart in regeneration (chap. 8); and the new sanctuary, with its Servant and service before God in heaven (chap. 9). It is now in order to present the basic and fundamental provision upon which all the above blessings depend. It is the provision of the one sacrifice, with its infinite and eternal efficacy to put away sin (chap. 10).

The argument for the efficacy of this one sacrifice proceeds through the first eighteen verses of the chapter, and is followed immediately by an appeal based directly upon the efficacy of this one sacrifice (10:19-39). In this chapter the fundamental of all fundamentals is argued and applied to these Hebrew Christians. This is the foundation for all Christianity, and it is therefore the fundamental truth to which countless numbers of professed Christians need to come today.

I. THE ARGUMENT FOR THE EFFICACY OF THE ONE SACRIFICE (10:1-18).

The key to this passage is in verse 12, "But this man, after he had offered one sacrifice for sins for ever, sat down on the right hand of God." To illuminate this fact, the writer contrasts the many sacrifices in Israel (vv. 1-4) with the one sacrifice of Christ (vv. 5-9), and then points to the consequences which issue from Christ's perfect sacrifice (vv. 10-18).

1. The *contrasts* are set forth in the imperfections of the many (vv. 1-4) and the perfections of the one (vv. 5-9).

The *imperfections* of the many are only what we might expect, but the clear statement of the Word of God confirms human reason (vv. 1-4). Those many sacrifices in Israel were *shadows and not substance* (v. 1), and shadows cannot make perfect. Shadows are only reflections cast from the real thing, and since they are not the real, it is only too evident that they cannot possibly provide spiritual blessing. Even the worshiper was aware of this, for his *conscience witnessed to imperfection* (v. 2). If there had been any power in those sacrifices to take away sin, they would have ceased to be offered. But no, the offering went on from year to year without end. And what is more, this continual offering was a *constant reminder of sin* (v. 3). Every year the bringing of another sacrifice pointed to the fact that the offering of the previous year did not take away sin, and so the worshiper was still in his sins. How depressing this must have been to those people. But the real imperfection of those offerings resided in the fact that they were *non-moral,* that is, it was animal blood that was offered (v. 4). And it is self-evident that such blood, though having symbolic value, cannot be finally efficacious on behalf of moral beings like men.

The *perfections* of the one sacrifice came as a balm to the weary offerer of long ago (vv. 5-9). The one sacrifice was a *sufficient sacrifice,* for it was the infinite God who made it. He came into the world He had made to offer this sacrifice (v. 5). It was also a *sinless sacrifice*, for the body (complete humanity) was fitted or made sound and complete (v. 5), and its sinlessness was demonstrated by His perfect life. It was also a *set sacrifice* in that God had pleasure in it, which was not true of the many sacrifices in Israel (v. 6). And what is even more interesting than the above, His was a *self-sacrifice* (vv. 7-9). The animals that were offered from year to year went unwillingly to slaughter. But the Lord Jesus Christ went willingly to the place of the skull. These four things make the one sacrifice of Christ absolutely perfect.

2. The *consequences* issuing from the one perfect sacri-

fice of Christ are four in number and avail for every believer in Christ (vv. 10-18).

The believer's *position in sin* was dealt with, for he was *sanctified* through the offering of the body of Jesus Christ once for all (v. 10). This sanctification was purely judicial, but it was perfect. It took the believer out of the realm of those who are classed as sinners and placed him in a class with those who are regarded as without sin. And the operation was final. There will be no fluctuations back and forth from one group to another. It is this sanctification which enables believers to be called saints.

The believer's obligation to suffer *penalty for sin* was also dealt with, because the one sacrifice for sins *justified him* (vv. 11-13). This, too, is a judicial operation on the part of God. It satisfied the law of God and cleared the sinner of the obligation to suffer the penalty demanded by the law. The one sacrifice so completely satisfied the law, as the many sacrifices could not do (v. 11), that when He finished with it, He sat down (v. 12). Now all He needs to do is wait for the issues from it (v. 13).

The believer's subjugation to the *power of sin* was dealt with, because as a result the worshipers are *regenerated* (vv. 15-16). Long ago the Holy Ghost promised that as a result of this offering, the new covenant would come in and the laws of God would be written upon the heart and in the mind. The new nature He would impart would make them to know righteousness and want to do it. And besides this, the new nature would give them the power to live lives of holiness (Phil. 2:12-13; I Thess. 4:7-8). This was translating into actual, personal experience, what could only remain a hope to the Old Testament worshiper.

The believer's *presence in sin* was also dealt with, for this one sacrifice *perfected* him forever (vv. 14, 17-18). In these verses we see the believer's life from the moment of faith until he enters the courts of glory where Christ is today. Since this one sacrifice took away even the remembrance of sins (v. 17), this meant that there was no longer need to repeat offerings (v. 18). Therefore, the end is certain. But the means to the end is progressive, personal sanctification, as stated by the words "are sanctified" (v. 14). More literally they read, "are being sanctified." This is the progressive setting aside from sin, which will one day be consummated and even the presence of sin will be done away (I John 3:2).

II. THE APPEAL BASED UPON THE EFFICACY OF THE ONE SACRIFICE (10:19-39).

The appeal follows the plan of setting forth the possibilities and responsibilities of believers (vv. 19-25), the perils which face those who apostatize (vv. 26-31), and the persistence needed to arrive at complete salvation (vv. 32-39).

1. The *possibilities and responsibilities* of believers (vv. 19-25). "Therefore" (v. 19) makes it clear that that which follows is based upon the facts which precede.

The *possibilities* of the believer are three in number (vv. 19-21). The *place* into which the believer may now enter is "the holiest" (v. 19). He may enter there boldly and without any fear of harm because he does so through the blood of Jesus. The veil has been rent and he can now come in before the face of God in prayer. The *way* into the holy of holies is new and living (v. 20). The word "new" means freshly slain and refers to the sacrifice of Christ; the word "living" means active and serving and refers to the priestly ministry of Christ. The *Priest* himself is the great High Priest, Christ, who is over the house of God (v. 21).

The *responsibilities* follow immediately and are introduced by the phrase "let us" (vv. 22-25). These responsibilities are *individual* (vv. 22-24) and *collective* (v. 25). They are individual first of all and include the obligation of drawing near to God (v. 22), holding fast our confession (v. 23), and considering one another (v. 24). The collective responsibility is negatively, "not forsaking the assembling of ourselves together," and positively, "exhorting one another: and so much the more, as ye see the day approaching" (v. 25).

2. The *perils* of those who knowingly and willingly apostatize (vv. 26-31). Following the plan he has used previously, the writer turns again to solemn exhortation and warning. Where there is great blessing, there is also great responsibility. And where this responsibility is shunned there is great punishment.

Rejecting Christ therefore brings *everlasting punishment* (vv. 26-27). Sinning willfully does not describe a mere deflection from the path. With such knowledge, such sinning is apostasy, a deliberate and persistent experience over a certain path of evil. For such people there remains nothing but fiery indignation.

Rejecting Christ brings *more severe punishment* than transgression of the law (vv. 28-29). Justice was done when one despised the law of Moses, and he suffered physical death (v. 28). But the punishment must be much greater when one treads under foot the Son of God, counts the blood unholy, and despises the Spirit of grace (v. 29).

Rejecting Christ will bring one into *inescapable punishment* (vv. 30-31). Vengeance, after all, belongs to the Lord, and He will judge His people. If anyone imagines that this is an idle threat, let him remember that the Lord is the living God, that is, He is active and able to perform all He promises. And it is fearful to fall into His hands.

3. The *persistence* needed to arrive at complete salvation

(vv. 32-39). This passage is a turn from warning to encouragement.

They had demonstrated persistence *in the past* (vv. 32-34). This followed their conversion (v. 32) and it was commendable. For they endured a great fight of afflictions, they were made a public spectacle, and they participated along with others in their distresses.

There was need for them to continue in persistence *in the present* (vv. 35-37). They are therefore encouraged not to cast away their boldness, for they have need of persistence, knowing the Coming One will not tarry.

Those who are truly Christian will continue in persistence *to the very end* (vv. 38-39). The just live by faith daily. Those who draw back have never come within divine pleasure.

QUESTIONS FOR DISCUSSION

1. What is the basic element in the provision of Christ that lays the foundation for all other blessings, according to chapter 10?

2. What is the movement of thought in this chapter, that is, what two main divisions are to be distinguished?

3. What are some of the imperfections of the Levitical sacrifices under the Old Testament covenant as set forth in verses 1-4?

4. What perfections center in the one sacrifice of Christ that make it superior to the Levitical sacrifices according to verses 5-9?

5. What does this one sacrifice of Christ accomplish in the believer according to verses 10-18?

6. What possibilities and responsibilities does this one sacrifice open up for the believer according to verses 19-25, and what perils according to verses 26-31?

11

The
Defense

The position of Christ has been set forth (chaps. 1-4); the perfection of Christ has been presented (chaps. 5-7); the provision of Christ has been declared (chaps. 8-10). It is now time to insist upon the possession of Christ (chaps. 11-13). In the final chapters of this epistle the writer draws his great defense of Christianity to a close by applying everything he has written to these Hebrew Christians. The position, perfection, and provision of Christ will go for nothing unless these people come into personal possession of Christ.

Possession of Christ involves three things: the appropriation of Christ through faith (chap. 11), the perseverance of faith in Christ (chap. 12), and the separation to Christ from the world (chap. 13). Chapter 11 is devoted to the primary responsibility of coming into possession of Christ, which is performed by faith. The constant recurrence of the word "faith" throughout the chapter is the key to its meaning. It may be divided into three parts: the description of faith (vv. 1-3), the operation of faith (vv. 4-38), and the perfection of faith (vv. 39-40).

I.   THE DESCRIPTION OF FAITH (11:1-3).

While there are some who insist that we have in these verses a definition of faith, if it is, it is a definition by description. The word "faith" itself is almost a definition, for it means "persuaded" or "persuasion." And so we may define faith by saying that it is the persuasion of the will based upon facts of knowledge concerning things that are not present to the senses. We shall note four things about faith as contained in the description of verses 1-3.

1. Faith is the *legal title* to unrealized possessions (v. 1). That is the meaning of the first clause, "Now faith is the substance of things hoped for." The word "substance" does not mean "assurance" as it has been rendered in some trans-

lations. Archaeological research reveals the fact that this word means *title deed.* "Things hoped for" are things not yet realized, but will be possessed at some time in the future. Faith is the title deed to these things.

2. Faith is the *legal evidence* of unseen possessions (v. 1). The last clause of the verse is now being considered, "the evidence of things not seen." The word "evidence" is a legal term describing evidence acceptable in a court. Such is the title deed. Though a man may never have seen the property he bought, if he has a title deed to it, that is evidence of its existence. And in the same manner, a believer may never have seen his mansions in the skies, but faith is his title deed, and the evidence that it really does exist.

3. Faith is the *legal procedure* for appropriating possessions (v. 2). "For by it the elders obtained a good report." This means that by it the elders were testified to by God as the worthy heirs of these possessions. God saw their faith and declared that they were the ones who would finally enter into the promises. And having seen their faith God also caused their faith to become in them a conviction that they would enter into the promised possessions.

4. Faith is the *legal method* of reaching ultimate reality (v. 3). That is the meaning of verse 3, "Through faith we understand that the worlds were framed by the word of God, so that things which are seen were not made of things which do appear." In this statement, the writer is affirming that nothing can be accounted for by an examination of itself. It is impossible to give careful study of the worlds and explain how they came into existence. By faith, however, one is able to reach out beyond the place where pure reason functions and determine for a certainty that the worlds were framed by the word of God. This does not mean that faith is opposed to

the exercise of the mind. It is quite to the contrary. Faith becomes an aid to the mind so that the understanding may reach its fullest possibilities. By means of faith, the understanding is able to reach ultimate reality.

II. THE OPERATION OF FAITH (11:4-38).

At this point the writer calls up all the witnesses to the value and worthwhileness of faith. From the very origin of mankind, right on down through the important years of the Jewish commonwealth, witness after witness is called to the stand to give his testimony. We see faith in operation in the old world (vv. 4-7), among the patriarchs (vv. 8-22), during the period of conquest (vv. 23-31), and during Israel's national life (vv. 32-38).

1. Faith in operation during *the old world,* and the testimony of the witnesses (vv. 4-7). Three great saints are called to the witness stand—Abel, Enoch, and Noah.

Abel *worshiped* by faith (v. 4). Faith was the motive which moved Abel, and the method by which Abel offered a more excellent sacrifice than Cain. Because of this faith he obtained witness that he was righteous and God testified of his gifts. And now even after the centuries have passed, by means of faith, even though dead, he yet speaks.

Enoch *walked* by faith (v. 5). In that evil day before the flood when men had turned their faces away from God, and lived as though there were no God, Enoch walked by faith. He walked on and on and on, and one day God said, "You are closer to My house than yours; come up with Me," and he "was translated that he should not see death."

Noah *worked* by faith (v. 7). In the midst of the unthinkable sin of the days before the flood God decided to preserve one man and his family through the judgment. Noah believed God and prepared an ark over a long period of time, and every nail he drove into the ark was another evidence of his faith that he believed God would destroy the world by water.

The writer cannot resist at this point to say something more about faith (v. 6). Without it, it is impossible to please God. For the one who comes to Him must be persuaded that He exists; and he must believe that God will reward those who diligently seek Him. If these things are not true, why exercise faith at all?

2. Faith in operation *among the patriarchs,* and the testimony of the witnesses (vv. 8-22). Such illustrious characters as Abraham (vv. 8-19), Isaac (v. 20), Jacob (v. 21), and Joseph (v. 22) come into view.

Abraham, as he set out for the city which hath foundations, and Sarah, as she became the mother of the promised seed, are drawn to the attention of these Hebrew Christians (vv. 8-19). They are being reminded that these founders of their own race entered into cooperative relationship with God by faith.

He again makes *a comment,* with consideration, before he goes on with the story of Abraham and Sarah (vv. 13-16). He declares that these died in faith without receiving the promise. For Abraham and Sarah this was a kingdom here in the earth. But their traveling on in faith was clear evidence that they did not intend to go back to the former things.

Isaac, Jacob, and *Joseph* also gave testimony to the fact that they belonged to the noble clan of faith (vv. 20-22). Though the experiences were different, yet the same principle of faith was in operation.

3. Faith was also in operation during the *period of conquest* (vv. 23-31). Moses, the great prophet, leader, and lawgiver, is the oustanding representative of that period (vv.

23-23). The faith of his mother spared him for a great task (v. 23). By his own choice he turned away from Egypt, with all it offered, to serve God (vv. 24-26). He might have one day been the Pharaoh of Egypt. But he turned his back upon it. By the exercise of the same faith he led the people forth from Egypt and kept the Passover (vv. 27-28). He endured as seeing Him who is invisible. Israel, under the leadership of Moses, exercised faith (vv. 29-30); and a harlot, Rahab, just as Israel was entering the land, exercised faith, and was brought into the royal lineage of Christ (v. 31).

4. Faith was in operation during the period of *Israel's national life* (vv. 32-38). At this point the writer gives place to an expression which tells just how he feels. "And what shall I more say?" He feels that he has said enough to settle the matter. After calling this many witnesses to the stand, surely the matter ought to be settled in the minds of his readers. Faith is worthwhile. Time is running out on the writer, and the multitude of witnesses available are almost without end. He does not dare let any of them tell their story. He can only mention their names—Gideon, Barak, Samson, Jephthae, David, Samuel (v. 32).

For the *sake of brevity*, he even refrains from giving names, in order to pay proper tribute to the triumphs that were won by faith, and the trials that were endured through faith (vv. 33-38). The nameless multitude which was borne to triumph on the wings of faith (vv. 33-35); what a story each one could tell. They subdued kingdoms, wrought righteousness, obtained promises, stopped the mouths of lions, quenched the violence of fire, escaped the edge of the sword, and won the many other victories marked up to their credit. Yes, and their endurance of trials through faith is equally valiant (vv. 36-38). It is thrilling to be delivered *out of* danger through faith; but how much more wonderful it is to be enabled to endure *through* trials. The mockings, scourgings, imprisonments, stonings, wanderings, and destitution were not taken away. In the midst of these the saints endured. Surely the writer is correct when he declares, "Of whom the world was not worthy" (v. 38).

III. THE PERFECTION OF FAITH (11:39-40).

At this point the writer places *a limitation* upon the thought of the passage. Although all these mighty witnesses to the value of faith have passed on, it is declared that they have not entered into the promises (v. 39). This does not have reference to the larger life of the spirit. Joy and peace and rest are theirs now. But they have not been perfected, and will not be until, in the times of God, Christians too are perfected in the kingdom to be established in the earth (v. 40).

QUESTIONS FOR DISCUSSION

1. To what practical purpose in the final three chapters of the Book of Hebrews has the writer devoted the first ten chapters of doctrine?

2. What is the key to chapter 11, and what does the writer hope to accomplish in emphasizing the key?

3. What is the definition of the word "faith," and what four things does the writer use to describe it?

4. What three men before the flood exercised faith, and what special thing is attributed to each one?

5. During the periods of the patriarchs, conquest, and national life of Israel, name those who were listed as the greatest?

6. Upon whom do the heroes of the faith wait for the fulfillment of promises as declared by the writer in the final two verses of the chapter?

12

Training Children

One by one the heroes and heroines in the army of the Lord have marched to the witness stand and have given unflinching and unequivocal testimony to the value of faith. The writer of this epistle is now ready to make the smashing application to his immediate audience. He is not suggesting that they do not have faith. Their own words were that they were intending to leave that faith and turn back to old Judaism. Therefore he has already insisted, "ye have need of patience [persistence]" (10:36) in faith. And now he says, "let us run with patience [persistence] the race" (12:1) of faith that is set before us. It is persistence, perseverance in faith like the heroes of old to which the writer now exhorts them.

With the idea in mind of encouraging these Hebrew Christians to continue on in the faith they have endorsed, the writer proceeds to the argument. He first presents the supreme example of perseverance in faith (vv. 1-4). He then outlines the many perils to perseverance (vv. 5-17). The great encouragement to perseverance is then given (vv. 18-24). And finally he delivers a stern appeal (vv. 25-29).

I. THE SUPREME EXAMPLE OF PERSEVERANCE IN FAITH (12:1-4).

This can be none other than the Lord Jesus Christ (v. 2). But before urging his readers to look to Him, he delivers his exhortation (v. 1), and following the example (v. 2), he points to the extremity (vv. 3-4) to which every believer should go.

1. The *exhortation* to perseverance (v. 1). The *predecessors* in this great race are that great cloud of witnesses that have gone on before (chap. 11). Each one by his life of faith has testified that persistence in faith is worthwhile. But if these Hebrew Christians expect to follow the witnesses, they

must make certain preparations for the running of this race. They must "lay aside every weight." This means anything that slackens the pace of the runner. For a runner, it means stripping down to essential clothing. But something far more important to the runner in this race is the next thing, namely, the laying aside of "the sin which doth so easily beset us." This sin is unbelief. It is the only sin that the writer has been constantly pointing out throughout this epistle.

There must also be included in the running of this race a *persistence* (patience), a perseverance, a dogged determination to win the race no matter what the odds may be. This running must be with the setting of the eye upon the goal, and a keeping of the eye upon it until the goal is reached. The *provision* of the race-contest, for such is the race, and such is the way it came to every believer, is a divine provision. One can see it in full when he looks at Christ. It starts in the earth and reaches into heaven, and it is beset with hardship and trials all along the way. It means not only continuous running, but agony, conflict, difficulty, and distress in the way. And since it leads to the courts of glory, is there anyone who will underestimate its value?

2. The *example* of perseverance (v. 2). The supreme and lonely figure of Jesus stands out above all others as we approach this point. The career He led, the compulsion He followed, the cross He endured, the computation He made, and the crown He now wears have no equal before, nor since, nor ever. How appropriate to encourage these faltering believers to be "looking unto Jesus."

The *career* of Christ is set forth by the words "author and finisher" of our faith. These words do not mean quite what they seem to mean. They really mean "pioneer and perfecter." And by dropping out the italicized word "our," we have "the pioneer and perfecter of faith." This means that Jesus is the supreme revelation of the power of faith. He began the race and has run it through to the very end, and is set down in heaven. The *compulsion* He felt was in the kingdom that was set before Him. But it meant that in this race He must persist through the *cross,* which experience shall never be fully known by men. But He made a *computation,* a careful analysis, and despised the shame for the glory which lay beyond. And as a final result He finished the race, and today enjoys the *crown* at the end of the way (2:9).

3. The *extremity* for perseverance (vv. 3-4). But unless the reader carefully diagnoses the extremity to which Christ went in perseverance, he will not be sufficiently challenged to persist through all that lies ahead. So the writer encourages the reader to *"consider"* Him that endured. He means that one should place Christ's experience alongside his own as an analogy and make close comparison. The *"contradiction* of sinners" against "himself" is the reading of the Amplified Version, but in the margin of the American Standard Version is a reading, "themselves," which draws back the veil and leads into the very heart of the mystery of His passion. The gainsaying of sinners against Christ was ultimately against themselves. And it ruined them. It was this agony which He endured. This is the mystery of His suffering.

How much in order now to *call* these Hebrew Christians to the very point of His suffering, and theirs. "Ye have not yet resisted unto blood, striving against sin" (v. 4). Indeed they had not. No one of them had gone as far as He. In fact there was not one of them, who was about to turn back, who thought of anything in his suffering except himself. And yet their sufferings were the same "contradiction of sinners against themselves," lost men who could not ruin believers, but would ultimately ruin themselves. If by some miracle of grace these Hebrew Christians could catch the passion of Christ they might yet "fill up that which is behind of the afflictions of Christ," as Paul so desired for himself (cf. Col. 1:24). Perseverance in faith must therefore go so far as to endure through affliction, even death, for the sake of the one who inflicts it.

II.   THE MANY PERILS TO PERSEVERANCE (12:5-17).

These perils operate in two spheres: that of chastening or child training (vv. 5-13), and character development (vv. 14-17).

1. *Chastening* (vv. 5-13). This is of God and it is the method by which He brings His children to the place where they display the peaceable fruit of righteousness (v. 11). But there are two ways by which God's chastening may lose its value and effectiveness. By *forgetfulness* of this fact chastening may fail to accomplish its purpose in the life of believers (vv. 5-6). And as these Hebrew Christians fell into distress and persecution from the world, they forgot that God was using this to bring blessing into their lives. So the writer calls them again to the recognition of their own Scriptures (Prov. 3:11-12). But even if they remembered this truth, and perhaps they did, their *failure to respond* properly would destroy the effect of chastening (vv. 7-13). Endurance or perseverance through chastening is the proper way to respond. It is the evidence that they are sons, and recognize that their Father is seeking to do them good.

2. *Character development* (vv. 14-17). While chastening is in a sense negative, because it is brought upon believers from without, character development is something that depends upon the believer himself and proceeds from within. It is therefore his responsibility to *follow* after certain things such as peace and holiness (v. 14); and what is more, it is his

business to take care lest he *fail or fall* short of the grace of God, lest any root of bitterness rise up and defile, or lest he profane or count common the precious things of the Lord (vv. 15-17).

III. THE GREAT ENCOURAGEMENT TO PERSEVER-ANCE (12:18-24).

This comes in the nature of a contrast, the final one, between the old covenant and the new.

1. The *old covenant* is set forth by a sevenfold description (vv. 18-21). It is perfectly clear that the whole of it is divinely ordained. But it was a material covenant. All the phrases indicate it—a mount, fire, blackness, darkness, tempest, sound of trumpet, voice of words. These transport one to Sinai and the ministration through Moses. And while all of these things were divinely appointed, it is evident that they appealed to the senses of men. The effect upon the Israelites was such that they called for an end of this (v. 19). And the reason was that they could not endure what was commanded (v. 20). It was so terrifying that even Moses was filled with fear (v. 21). All this marked the ultimate failure of the first covenant because of men.

2. But the *new covenant*, how different, which is now given a sevenfold description (vv. 22-24). The writer now turns the mind of the reader from shadow to substance, from the symbolic to the real, from the failing to the successful. This is Mount Zion, the "company of angels," the "church of the firstborn," "God the Judge of all," "the spirits of just men made perfect," "Jesus the mediator of the new covenant," and "the blood of sprinkling." Every one of these speaks better things than the symbolism of the former covenant. And into these things men of faith have already en-

tered. This is reason for perseverance in this faith.

IV. THE STERN APPEAL TO PERSEVERANCE (12:25-29).

In this passage the writer takes his readers back to the very beginning. "God, who . . . spake in time past . . . hath in these last days spoken unto us by his Son" (1:1-2). "See that ye refuse not him that speaketh" (12:25). And there are five good reasons why this final word in the Son should not be refused. First, because the one who uttered it is *inescapable* in execution of wrath (v. 25). Second, because the one who uttered it is *universal* in the scope of His work (v. 26). Third, because the one who uttered it is *eternal* in the effect He produces (v. 27). Fourth, because the one who uttered it offers an *immovable* kingdom (v. 28). And finally, because the one who spoke is *fearful* in punishment (v. 29).

QUESTIONS FOR DISCUSSION

1. In view of the fact that the writer recognizes the real need of those to whom he writes (10:36), what does he now urge these Hebrew Christians to do?

2. In what sense were all the Old Testament heroes of faith referred to in trying to reach these Hebrew Christians?

3. Who is the supreme example of perseverance in faith, and to what extreme did He go in the exercise of faith?

4. There are perils to perseverance in faith, but in what two ways does God use these for the benefit of the believer?

5. What is the great encouragement for perseverance in faith in the new covenant, as over against the terrifying aspects of the old covenant?

6. What are some of the reasons given why the final word of God in Christ to men should not be refused?

13

In All
Your Walk

The final movement in the argument of this epistle is now before us. It is the finishing touch to the writer's appeal that these Hebrew Christians should enter into, and continue in, personal possession of Christ. This must be done by separation from the world, to Christ. If they are willing to "go forth therefore unto him without the camp, bearing his reproach" (13:13), then they will display for themselves and for others the crowning evidence that they have entered into saving relationship with Him, and they will seal to themselves the security of this salvation.

Separation is therefore the theme of this chapter. And it is something that should manifest itself in three spheres: in social conduct (vv. 1-6), in religious conduct (vv. 7-17), and in personal conduct (vv. 18-25). Just as faith was the means by which one made appropriation of Christ (chap. 11), and in which perseverance should take place (chap. 12), it is also the method by which separation from the world is to be effected (chap. 13).

I. SEPARATION FROM THE WORLD IN SOCIAL CONDUCT (13:1-6).

Social conduct is the relation of the individual to society. And the character of the conduct will depend upon the relationship of the individual to God. Since believers are children of God, it follows that the conduct they display should be altogether different from the conduct displayed by the children of this world. This will include conduct toward others (vv. 1-3), and toward self (vv. 4-6).

1. Social conduct directed toward *others in society* (vv. 1-3). The sons of God (v. 1), strangers (v. 2), and sufferers (v. 3), come within the vision of the writer.

Toward the *brethren*, brotherly love should continue (v. 1). The word "brotherly" implies the family relationship.

Where God the Father is the progenitor, and each child therefore has the same spiritual nature, and is moving toward the same destined end and goal, it is only right that love should be displayed mutually toward one another. And this love, as the original indicates, should be a warm, personal affection. There should be in it that intimacy which takes delight in, and finds attractiveness in, the object of affection. The writer is not suggesting by this command that they are not doing this very thing. He is rather urging them to let it go on.

Toward *strangers,* hospitality should be shown (v. 2). This is also a type of love. Quite literally the word "entertain" means "love strangers." It means to find some delight or attractiveness in strangers so that one will be impelled to do them good. While this injunction was particularly adapted to the times, the situation has not materially changed. It is the one way to display a heart for others not of one's own house. For one man in the past it meant the entertaining of angels (Gen. 18). No one ever knows who the recipient may be, nor what he may become as a result of a little love shown toward him.

Toward *sufferers,* deep sympathy should be shown (v. 3). Suffering among all men of that day is not out of mind as the writer proceeds. But perhaps he has especially in mind the suffering of the saints. Many were going to prison for their faith and others were suffering untold adversity of one kind or another (10:32-34). Each saint needed to keep in mind that he too might shortly be in the same circumstances. And how encouraging it would be if some one of the saints would display the same toward him.

2. Social conduct directed toward *himself in society* (vv. 4-6). Self-respect (v. 4), self-control (v. 5), and simple trust in God need discussion here.

Self-respect on the part of every believer needs attention

(v. 4). Marriage, which is so individual and personal, is a divinely ordained institution and is therefore to be regarded with the highest honor. Therefore all of the false ideas propagated in the earth, which ideas have done so much to pollute and pervert this holy institution, should be shunned. The marriage bed is to be regarded as clean and holy and legitimate. But those who pervert the sexual union and indulge in sexual vices God will judge. This, then, is a safeguard of the home.

Self-control is another virtue which needs cultivation (v. 5). Covetousness is the insatiable greed to be constantly acquiring more possessions. It grows out of the idea that our primary means of support is in things, and this issues in a lack of trust in God. Contentment is fostered by trust in God and no anxiety for the future.

Simple trust is the real answer to all covetousness (v. 6). Trust is that absolute persuasion of the heart that God will care for His own. A trusting soul therefore thinks of God from moment to moment as his helper. And no matter what the changes in society about him, no matter what men may do to him, no matter whether men dispossess him, he need not fear, for the Lord is his ultimate stay and support.

II. SEPARATION FROM THE WORLD IN RELIGIOUS CONDUCT (13:7-17).

It must not be forgotten that this epistle is especially concerned with Hebrew Christians in danger of returning to old Judaism. But Judaism, though divinely ordained for its day, had served its purpose and had passed away so far as being longer used of God. Therefore, to go back to Judaism was the same as going back into the world, for it was now of the world. Doctrine (vv. 7-9), worship (vv. 10-15), and leaders (vv. 16-17), fall within the realm of this discussion.

1. There should be *steadfastness in doctrine* (vv. 7-9). The *pastors* whom the Lord had placed over this people had been teaching them sound doctrine (v. 7). And it was their responsibility to remember these ruling saints and the word they spoke. And if there was any doubt in their minds about their message, all they need do is observe carefully the manner of life they were living, and its end. Life usually corresponds with doctrine. The great *Person* who is the sum and substance of the gospel message, is the same yesterday, today, and forever (v. 8). The doctrine about Him, therefore, cannot change. It is therefore the *responsibility* of believers not to be carried about with divers and strange doctrines (v. 9). The doctrines of old Judaism led up to and were fulfilled in Christ, and then passed away. And no turning back to the old forms can bring any profit to anyone, just as it brought no profit to the heart of the Old Testament worshipers.

2. There should be *separation from the world in worship* (vv. 10-15). The explanation for separation in worship (vv. 10-12) is followed by the exhortation to the same (vv. 13-15).

The *explanation* for separation in worship is confusing to the English reader, but it was perfectly clear to Hebrew Christians (vv. 10-12). The truth about the *altar* (v. 10) is not clearly stated in the English. Verse 10 is not intended to present a contrast between Christianity and Judaism. It is really a statement about Judaism, which is a type of Christian truth. The verse should read, "There is an altar whereof they have no right to eat which serve the tabernacle." And the context makes clear what the writer means. He is talking about the sin offering. It was not slain or offered at the altar. It was slain without the camp (v. 11), and it was not eaten. Every bit of it was burned. So just as there was no altar for the sin offering in Israel, there is none in Christianity. Just as the sin offering was killed and burned *without* the camp in the long ago (v. 11), so also Christ as the fulfillment of the type suffered without the gate. His suffering outside the gate indicated that the curse of God and the reproach of the people were upon Him (v. 12).

The *exhortation* for separation logically follows (vv. 13-15). This is the climax in the many exhortations to these Hebrew Christians. In the Old Testament covenant the camp was the arrangement of the Hebrew tribes in the wilderness, with the Tabernacle in the very center, and God dwelling in the most holy place. The sin offering was taken outside, for the curse of God was upon it in type, and the people showed their reproach for their own sins by their reproach for the sin offering. The exact type then was fulfilled in Christ. He suffered outside the gate in order that He might redeem the people within. If then the people of Israel expect to share in the salvation which is in Christ, then they must go outside the camp bearing His reproach. He was rejected by Israel and thrust outside of the camp. Those on the inside must go on the outside and share His reproach in order that they may enter into the salvation He bought. Within the camp of Israel there is no continuing city. And if one seeks such a city, he must follow Christ outside, and into the very holy of holies in heaven, the eternal city (v. 14).

This means that the believer not only has the privilege to enter into the holy of holies in heaven to worship, but it is his obligation to go there for worship, for there is where his High Priest is today. He may go there continually to offer the sacrifice of praise, the fruit of his lips.

3. There should be separation by way of *submission to leaders* (vv. 16-17). This too is closely associated with worship. Doing good and sharing material goods, the writer de-

clares, take the form of spiritual sacrifices which are offered in the holy of holies in heaven (v. 16). And this is especially true with respect to the attitude believers show toward their pastors. These pastors are doing their best to lead them to realize to the fullest extent the spiritual provision in Christ. Cooperation by way of submission is necessary to the best worship of Christ.

III. SEPARATION FROM THE WORLD IN PERSONAL CONDUCT (13:18-25).

The writer appeals for prayer for him (vv. 18-19); he responds with prayer for them (vv. 20-21); he urges them to receive counsel (vv. 22-23); and concludes with salutations and benediction (vv. 24-25).

QUESTIONS FOR DISCUSSION

1. What is the theme of chapter 13, and why is this the concluding and final step required of these Hebrew Christians if they were to have the assurance of possession of Christ?

2. In what three spheres should separation from the world be displayed on the part of true Christians?

3. How does conduct toward others in society and conduct of oneself display the fact that he is related to Christ and belongs to the family of the redeemed?

4. In the argument of verses 7-9, how does the writer establish the fact that there should be steadfastness of doctrine among believers?

5. In the light of the fact that Christ suffered without the camp, what does this mean for those who profess Christ if they truly want to be joined to Him?

6. In view of the fact that God has appointed leaders for the people, how should the people respond toward their leaders?

Bibliography

INTRODUCTION

Guthrie, Donald. *New Testament Introduction: Hebrews to Revelation.* Chicago: Inter-Varsity Press, 1964.

Harrison, Everett F. *Introduction to the New Testament.* Grand Rapids: Eerdmans Publishing Company, 1964.

Manley, G. T. *The New Bible Handbook.* London: Intervarsity Christian Fellowship, 1953.

Rees, T. *International Standard Bible Encyclopedia: Epistle to the Hebrews.* Chicago: Howard Severance Company, 1925. pp. 1355-1362.

Scroggie, W. Graham. *Know Your Bible, Vol. II, Analytical, The New Testament.* London: Pickering and Inglis, 1957.

Tenney, Merrill G. *The New Testament, A Survey.* Grand Rapids: Eerdmans Publishing Company, 1953.

Thiessen, Henry C. *Introduction to the New Testament.* Grand Rapids: Eerdmans Publishing Company, 1943.

Unger, Merrill F. *Bible Handbook.* Chicago: Moody Press, 1966.

ON THE GREEK TEXT

Alford, Henry. *The Greek Testament.* London: Beighton, Bell and Company, 1880.

Bruce, F. F. *The New International Commentary on the New Testament: Epistle to the Hebrews.* Grand Rapids: Eerdmans Publishing Company, 1970.

Calvin, John. *Commentaries on the Epistle of Paul to the Hebrews.* Grand Rapids: Eerdmans Publishing Company, 1948.

Delitzsch, Franz. *Commentary on the Epistle to the Hebrews.* Edinburgh: T. and T. Clark, 1870.

Dods, Marcus. *The Expositor's Greek Testament: Hebrews.* New York: George H. Doran Company, n. d.

Lenski, R. C. H. *Interpretation of Hebrews and James.* Columbus, Ohio: The Wartburg Press, 1938.

Lunemann, Gottlieb. *Meyer's Commentary on the New Testament: Hebrews.* New York: Funk and Wagnalls, 1890.

Owen, John. *An Exposition of the Epistle to the Hebrews.* Boston: Samuel T. Armstrong, 1811.

Rendall, Frederic. *Epistle to the Hebrews.* London: Macmillan and

Company, 1883.

Robertson, A. T. *Word Pictures in the New Testament.* New York: Ray Long and Richard R. Smith, 1932.

Sampson, Francis S. *A Critical Commentary on the Epistle to the Hebrews.* New York: Robert Carter and Brothers, 1856.

Schneider, Johannes. *The Letter to the Hebrews.* Grand Rapids: Eerdmans Publishing Company, 1957.

Stuart, Moses. *Commentary on the Epistle to the Hebrews.* New York: Flagg, Gould, and Newman, 1833.

Westcott, Brooke Foss. *Epistle to the Hebrews.* London: Macmillan and Company, 1909.

ENGLISH EXPOSITION

Anderson, Sir Robert. *The Hebrews Epistle.* London: Pickering and Inglis, n. d.

Archer, Gleason L. *The Epistle to the Hebrews.* Grand Rapids: Baker Book House, 1957.

Barnes, Albert. *Epistle to the Hebrews.* New York: Harper and Brothers, 1950.

Baxter, J. Sidlow. *Explore the Book: Hebrews.* Grand Rapids: Zondervan Publishing House, 1972.

Bruce, A. B. *The Epistle to the Hebrews.* Edinburgh: T. and T. Clark, 1899.

Bullinger, F. W. *The Great Cloud of Witnesses.* London: The Lamp Press, 1956.

Chadwick, G. A. *A Devotional Commentary on Hebrews.* London: Religious Tract Society, n. d.

Dale, R. W. *The Jewish Temple and the Christian Church.* London: Hodder and Stoughton, 1871.

Davidson, A. B. *Handbooks for Bible Classes: Hebrews.* Edinburgh: T. and T. Clark, n. d.

English, E. Schuyler. *Studies in the Epistle to the Hebrews.* Findlay, Ohio: Dunham Publishing Company, 1955.

Erdman, Charles R. *The Epistle to the Hebrews.* Philadelphia: The Westminster Press, 1934.

Farrar, F. W. *Cambridge Bible: Epistle to the Hebrews.* London: University Press, 1883.

Grant, F. W. *Notes on the Epistle to the Hebrews.* New York: Loizeaux

Brothers, n. d.

Hawthorne, Gerald F. *A New Testament Commentary:* Hebrews. Grand Rapids: Zondervan Publishing House, 1969.

Ironside, H. A. *Hebrews and Titus.* New York: Loizeaux Brothers, 1932.

Kent, Homer A., Jr. *The Epistle to the Hebrews.* Grand Rapids: Baker Book House, 1972.

Lang, G. H. *The Epistle to the Hebrews.* London: The Paternoster Press, 1951.

Macaulay, J. C. *Devotional Studies in the Epistle to the Hebrews.* Grand Rapids: Eerdmans Publishing Company, 1948.

Mauro, Philip. *God's Pilgrims.* London: Samuel E. Roberts, 1912.

Meyer, F. B. *The Way Into the Holiest.* London: Morgan and Scott, n. d.

Michelsen, A. Berkeley. *The Biblical Expositor: Hebrews.* Philadelphia: A. J. Holman Company, 1960.

Milligan, George. *The Theology of the Epistle to the Hebrews.* Edinburgh: T. and T. Clark, 1930.

Morgan, G. Campbell. *God's Last Word to Man.* New York: Fleming H. Revell Company, 1936.

_____. *The Analyzed Bible, The New Testament: Hebrews.* London: Hodder and Stoughton, 1908.

_____. *Living Messages of the Books of the Bible: Hebrews.* New York: Fleming H. Revell Company, 1912.

_____. *An Exposition of the Whole Bible: Hebrews.* Westwood, New Jersey: Fleming H. Revell Company, 1959.

_____. *Westminster Bible Conference 1911: The Letter to the Hebrews.* London: Morgan and Scott, n. d.

Moule, Handley G. C. *Messages from the Epistle to the Hebrews.* London: Thynne and Company, 1930.

Murray, Andrew. *The Holiest of All.* London: Nisbet and Company, n. d.

Nairne, Alexander. *The Epistle of Priesthood.* Edinburgh: T. and T. Clark, 1913.

Newell, William R. *Hebrews Verse by Verse.* Chicago: Moody Press, 1947.

Pettingill, William L. *Into the Holiest.* Findlay, Ohio: Fundamental Truth Publishers, 1939.

Pink, Arthur W. *An Exposition of Hebrews*. Swengel, Pennsylvania: Bible Truth Depot, 1954.

Ridout, Samuel. *Lectures on the Epistle to the Hebrews*. New York: Loizeaux Brothers, 1903.

Saphir, Adolph. *Epistle to the Hebrews*. New York: Gospel Publishing House, 1902.

Seiss, Joseph A. *Lectures on Hebrews*. Grand Rapids: Baker Book House, 1954.

Thomas, W. H. Griffith. *Let Us Go On*. Grand Rapids: Zondervan Publishing House, 1944.

Vine, W. E. *The Epistle to the Hebrews*. London: Oliphants Limited, 1957.

Vos, Geerhardus. *The Teaching of the Epistle to the Hebrews*. Grand Rapids: Eerdmans Publishing Company, 1956.

Wall, I. R. *Saved to the Uttermost*. New York: Fleming H. Revell Company, 1943.

Wiley, H. Orton. *Epistle to the Hebrews*. Kansas City: Beacon Hill Press, 1959.

Wuest, Kenneth S. *Hebrews in the Greek New Testament*. Grand Rapids: Eerdmans Publishing Company, 1947.

ADDITIONAL STUDY GUIDES IN THIS SERIES . . .

GENESIS, John P. Burke
EXODUS, Tom Julien
DEUTERONOMY, Bernard N. Schneider
JOSHUA, JUDGES & RUTH, John J. Davis
1 & 2 SAMUEL & 1 KINGS 1-11, John J. Davis
KINGS & CHRONICLES, John C. Whitcomb
JOB THROUGH SONG OF SOLOMON, Gerald H. Twombly
PROVERBS, Charles W. Turner
DANIEL, Robert D. Culver
THE MINOR PROPHETS, Gerald H. Twombly
MATTHEW, Harold H. Etling
MARK, Homer A. Kent, Jr.
GOSPEL OF JOHN, Homer A. Kent, Jr.
ACTS, Homer A. Kent, Jr.
ROMANS, Herman A. Hoyt
1 CORINTHIANS, James L. Boyer
2 CORINTHIANS, Homer A. Kent, Jr.
GALATIANS, Homer A. Kent, Jr.
EPHESIANS, Tom Julien
PHILIPPIANS, David L. Hocking
COLOSSIANS AND PHILEMON, Homer A. Kent, Jr.
1 & 2 TIMOTHY, Dean Fetterhoff
HEBREWS, Herman A. Hoyt
JAMES, Roy R. Roberts
1, 2, 3 JOHN, Raymond E. Gingrich
REVELATION, Herman A. Hoyt
THE WORLD OF UNSEEN SPIRITS, Bernard N. Schneider
THE HOLY SPIRIT AND YOU, Bernard N. Schneider
PROPHECY, THINGS TO COME, James L. Boyer
PULPIT WORDS TRANSLATED FOR PEW PEOPLE, Charles W. Turner
SWEETER THAN HONEY, Jesse B. Deloe *(A guide to effective Bible study and the background of how we got our Bible)*
BRETHREN BELIEFS AND PRACTICES, Harold H. Etling
THE FAMILY FIRST, Kenneth O. Gangel
LESSONS IN LEADERSHIP FROM THE BIBLE, Kenneth O. Gangel

Obtain from your local Christian bookstore or request an order blank from BMH Books, P. O. Box 544, Winona Lake, Ind. 46590